Using Science Notebooks
in Elementary Classrooms

By: Michael P. Klentschy

Using Science Notebooks
in Elementary Classrooms

Michael P. Klentschy

NATIONAL SCIENCE TEACHERS ASSOCIATION

Arlington, Virginia

Claire Reinburg, Director
Judy Cusick, Senior Editor
Andrew Cocke, Associate Editor
Betty Smith, Associate Editor

ART AND DESIGN
Will Thomas, Jr., Art Director
Joseph Butera, Graphic Designer—Cover and Inside Design

PRINTING AND PRODUCTION
Catherine Lorrain, Director
Nguyet Tran, Assistant Production Manager
Jack Parker, Electronic Prepress Technician

National Science Teachers Association
Gerald F. Wheeler, Executive Director
David Beacom, Publisher

Library of Congress Cataloging-in-Publication Data

Klentschy, Michael P.
  Using science notebooks in elementary classrooms / by Michael P. Klentschy.
     p. cm.
  Includes bibliographical references and index.
  ISBN 978-1-933531-03-8
  1. Science--Study and teaching (Elementary) 2. Language arts--Correlation with content subjects. 3.
School notebooks. I. Title.
  LB1585.K54 2008
  372.3'5044--dc22
                          2008004612

  eISBN 978-1-935155-40-9

Contents

Contents

i. Introduction

In an era of standards, assessment, and accountability, increased demands are placed on students to demonstrate an understanding of science content and on teachers to assess and determine the depth of student understanding. One of the major goals of elementary science instruction in this context is the development of scientific literacy in students. The American Association for the Advancement of Science (1993) recommends that scientific literacy involve student ability to determine relevant from irrelevant information, explain and predict scientific events, and link claims to evidence to make scientific arguments. The National Research Council (2000) also recommends that both student knowledge and content understanding be included in the assessment of science outcomes. Furthermore, the National Research Council (1999, 2005) recommends that instructional planning and classroom instruction focus on maximizing student opportunity to learn. Teachers can do this when planning, instruction, and assessment focuses on the following three principles:

(1) Engage students to activate prior knowledge.

(2) To develop competence in an area of inquiry, students

    a. must have a deep foundation of factual knowledge;

    b. must understand facts in the context of conceptual frameworks; and

    c. must organize knowledge in ways that facilitate retrieval and application.

(3) Recognize that metacognitive approaches to instruction can help students take control of their own learning by defining goals and monitoring their progress.

In addressing these three principles in instructional planning, teachers must also determine appropriate methods to assess student progress. These three principles align to a model of metacognition developed by Glynn and Muth (1994). In this model, students develop metacognitive ability through learning science by accessing prior science content knowledge; using science-process skills; and applying reading, writing, listening, and speaking skills to learn content. In using this model to address the three principles, student science notebooks and class discussion may be effective assessment tools for teachers.

Songer and Ho (2005) identify three challenges of instructional programs that foster student development of scientific inquiry. These challenges focus on the development of reasoning skills closely aligned to scientific literacy:

(1) the formulation of scientific explanations from evidence (and the actual linking of claims to evidence);

Introduction

(2) analysis of various types of scientific data (evidence); and

(3) the formulation of conclusions based upon relevant evidence.

Classroom teachers can assist students in developing these reasoning skills by carefully crafting the use of science notebooks as part of their classroom science instruction. This includes specific instruction through the use of scaffolds, sentence starters, and prompts. The science notebook then becomes a thinking tool for the student. The application of language arts is essential for students not only to develop a deep understanding of science content but also to attain scientific literacy.

Science may be the perfect content area to integrate language arts, particularly expository writing in the form of student science notebooks. Student science notebooks have proven to be the best record of what science content is actually taught and learned and provides an excellent ongoing assessment and feedback tool for teachers (Ruiz-Primo et al. 2002). Students should be provided with the opportunity to write to themselves as an audience in their science notebooks and not to the teacher as an audience. This is the development of the concept of "voice" by the student and provides specific data to teachers of student conceptual understanding. Students thinking and making meaning from science instruction through their science notebooks has led to increased student achievement in not only science but reading and writing as well (Amaral et al. 2002; Klentschy and Molina-De La Torre 2004; Vitale et al. 2005). As such, a science notebook becomes a central place where language, data, and experience operate jointly to form meaning for the student. The development of "voice" is a process that takes place over time and is enhanced with specific teacher feedback (Amaral et al. 2002; Jorgenson and Vanosdall 2002; Ruiz- Primo et al. 2002; Saul et al. 2002).

Student science notebooks, used well, not only provide opportunities for students to develop a deeper conceptual understanding of science, but also address other issues faced by classroom teachers today, most notably time, through the integration of language arts and science when typically only reading and mathematics are taught in many classrooms (Klentschy 2006).

Students' written ideas provide a window into their thinking process. The science notebook then can be viewed as a tool utilized by students during their science experiences and investigations

National Science Teachers Association

and in social interactions with group members and the class, as a tool for personal reflection, and as a tool for constructing personal meaning of the science content being studied. The science notebook has been a tool used by scientists to help them in the same regard.

Many classroom teachers use student science notebooks as a regular part of their classroom instruction in science. Some teachers have a systematic approach for their use, while some do not. Many teachers who are not using student science notebooks would like to but are not sure exactly how to start or even what format the notebooks should follow.

This book is designed to assist classroom teachers who are currently using student science notebooks as a part of their classroom science instruction by providing them with a systematic research-based approach to extend and to either reinforce or build upon what they are presently doing. This book is also designed to assist classroom teachers who may just be getting started or wish to start using student science notebooks in their classrooms. Research-based best practices such as scaffolds, sentence starters, discussion starters, and writing prompts are included to build upon existing knowledge. Numerous examples of student work are provided to help both categories of teachers develop insight into instructional strategies for their classrooms. A discussion of the needs of English language learners is provided with specific strategies to increase both their language fluency and writing proficiency. Finally, research-based practices to use student science notebooks as an effective assessment tool are provided through scoring guides and other approaches to providing student feedback to both underline the importance of feedback to students and after some classroom-tested ways to do it.

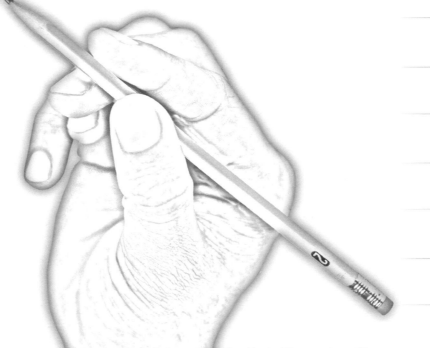

CHAPTER 1

What Do We Know About Writing and Science?

Science is the perfect content area to integrate language arts, particularly expository writing in the form of student science notebooks. Student science notebooks have also proven to be the best record of what science content is actually taught by teachers in classrooms and learned by students and provide an excellent ongoing assessment and feedback tool for teachers (Ruiz-Primo et al. 2002).

Many educators hold the belief that student science notebooks are a very special, essential means of communication. This belief centers on the notion that the act of writing by its very nature enhances thinking by demanding that the student organize language. Student science notebooks used well provide not only stability and permanence to student's work but also purpose and form. They become a record of personally valued information. This form of writing may also help students link new information

What Do We Know About Writing and Science?

with prior knowledge (Rivard 1994) and provide a reflective opportunity for students to develop a deeper understanding of science content.

Communication has a central role around the process of inquiry. Communication is a vital aspect of the process of science. Students need to have a place and a means to reflect on their ideas. Language becomes the primary avenue that students use to arrive at scientific understanding. Student science notebooks become the means for students to apply language and reflect on their ideas.

The key to effective science teaching is to enable students to develop ideas about the world around them from evidence that they have collected and developed personal meaning. Learning science involves both the process of thinking and the ability to communicate those thoughts.

By linking science and language literacy through student science notebooks, teachers can demonstrate the role of science in strengthening language skills, thus extending and strengthening the place of science in the curriculum. Learning science helps children develop an understanding of the world around them. For this, students have to build up concepts that help them link their experiences together and learn ways of collecting and organizing information and of applying and testing new ideas. This learning not only contributes to children's ability to make better sense of the world around them but also helps develop their decision-making and problem-solving skills.

Learning involves both a personal and social construction of meaning. In the classroom, students become agents of their own learning, constructing scientific concepts by drawing on their existing ideas and experience; social interactions mediate knowledge construction and knowledge is personally constructed (Shepardson and Britsch 2001). Learning science also involves students being able to communicate their thinking. This form of communication is oral, written, and symbolic in the form of drawings. Vygotsky (1978) concluded that personally meaningful knowledge is socially constructed through shared understandings.

Science and literacy also have another strong point of connection through the desire of many educators to develop metacognitive awareness in children. Metacognition often takes the form of an internal dialogue. Many students may be unaware of its importance unless teachers explicitly emphasize the processes. Research has demonstrated that children can be taught these strategies, including the ability to predict outcomes, explain oneself in order to improve understanding, note failures to understand, and to plan ahead (NRC 1999).

In order to examine the utility of student science notebooks for assessment, it is important to examine the context that student science notebooks play in an inquiry-based program of science instruction. Children construct models of the workings of written language by interaction with people and objects in their environment.

They simultaneously construct understandings of science phenomena that may be reflected in both their writing and drawing (White and Gundstone 1992). This view establishes a foundation for a teaching approach wherein children learn science by doing science and use writing as part of their science experiences. In the context of science activities, student-produced science notebooks promote the use of scientific literacy while clarifying students' emerging understanding about science content.

The use of writing as a vehicle to promote learning is consistent with the belief that the writer is engaged in active reprocessing at the level of concepts and central ideas (Scardamalia and Bereiter 1986). Writing enables students to express their current ideas about science content in a form that they can examine and think about. The first goal of writing is to understand. Writing is an instrument to think with. Written words provide cues for expressing ideas verbally to others. Achievement in science is directly proportional to the student's ability to use language (Fellows 1994).

Student science notebooks are a student's personal record, an extension of their mental activities, and a store of personally valued information. Science notebooks can also contain drawings, tables, or graphs that are essential in forming meaning from the science experience. The earlier children start to learn to keep records, the better they will be prepared to make this a natural part of their science activities. Children will recognize this from experiences that require them to collect and interpret times and distances or data on other measurements. The use of student science notebooks in class discussions helps students construct meaning of the science phenomena (Rivard and Straw 2000). Many teachers begin the use of student science notebooks as early as kindergarten.

The student science notebook then becomes more than a record of data that students collect, facts they learn, and procedures they conduct. The science notebook also becomes a record of students' reflections, questions, speculations, decisions and conclusions all focused on the science phenomena. As such, a science notebook becomes a central place where language, data, and experience operate jointly to form meaning for the student.

Vygotsky (1978) referred to drawing as graphic speech and noted that young students' representations often reflect what they know about the object more that what is actually perceived. These drawings can act as a guide to students' understandings. Students incorporate different selections of such details in order to draw the experience into a context that makes sense to them. Drawing and writing produced in a science investigation are valuable because they allow students to express their ideas and findings; they take the role of talk with regard to assisting students in making meaning of their ideas. Classroom teachers should view the use of student drawings as an important aspect in developing the science-literacy connection.

What Do We Know About Writing and Science?

Discrete knowledge should not be learned for its own sake. Students should be challenged to use this knowledge in solving meaningful problems. Student science notebooks can serve as the medium for fleshing out responses to complex problems requiring higher-order reasoning. The way that writing is employed and evaluated in the classroom is critical in determining students' perceptions of its potential for learning content (Rivard 1994). By creating their own science notebook pages, students are able to describe their ways of seeing and thinking about the science phenomena, constructing and reconstructing meaning through their own lens of experience (Shepardson and Britsch 2001).

The nature of students' contextualization of science phenomena and the activity on the science notebook page are dependent on the students' familiarity with the phenomena and equipment and length of exposure to the program of instruction (Amaral et al. 2002). In unfamiliar situations, entries reflect and describe the immediately observed science investigation, whereas in familiar situations the children's entries are based on their experiences with the phenomena, placing the science investigation into a real-world context (Shepardson 1997). In an analysis of the initial use of student science notebooks in Imperial County, California, the students' first science notebooks took on the form of a narrative or procedural recount (Amaral et al. 2002). Writing is developmental and teachers must guide students to be more reflective about their work. Student science notebooks have the potential to move students beyond simply completing the task to making sense of the task.

The developmental movement from writing about what was done during the science investigation to writing about what was learned during the science investigation is assisted by embedding writing prompts into the inquiry process. It may be equally important for students to learn how to use science notebooks as a means to create a permanent record of the classroom science investigations. Carefully developed writing prompts for student writing in classroom science instruction may enhance student science content understanding for standards-based instructional units.

These embedded writing prompts are based on the lessons learned from the Valle Imperial Project in Science from 1996–2004 (Klentschy and Molina-De La Torre 2004; Klentschy 2005; and Amaral et al. 2006). It is believed that writing may force the integration of new ideas and relationships with prior knowledge and encourage personal involvement with new information (Kleinsasser et al. 1992). Student science notebooks then become an extended opportunity for students to explain, describe, predict, and integrate new information, and allow students to make conceptual shifts and facilitate retention. The use of embedded writing prompts provides students with extended opportunities to learn how to write in their science notebooks. Students benefit from the use of these writing prompts with respect to building explanations from evidence (Songer 2003). Questioning, predicting, clarifying, and summarizing are strengthened through the use of embedded writing prompts. Clarifying promotes comprehension monitoring.

Writing prompts help students analyze data and build explanations from evidence (Hug et al. 2005). A process of guided inquiry, reflection, and generalization develops students' metacognitive knowledge (White and Fredrickson 1998). Writing is an important tool for transforming claims and evidence into knowledge that is more coherent and structured and appears to enhance the retention of science learning over time (Rivard and Straw 2000). These research-based findings are closely aligned to the recommendations for teaching science by the National Research Council (2005) and are aligned to how students can develop a deep understanding of science content.

CHAPTER 2

What Is a Science Notebook?

Student science notebooks are advocated by researchers who believe that writing in science enhances student understanding of science content and process skills (Amaral et al. 2002; Campbell and Fulton, 2003; Klentschy and Molina-De La Torre 2004; Rivard and Straw 2000; Shepardson and Britsch 2001). Student science notebooks can be embedded into the science curriculum as a natural part of the goal to assist students in making evidence-based explanations of their science investigations.

The student science notebook is more than a record of data that students collect, facts they learn, and procedures they conduct. It is also a record of students' reflections, questions, predictions, claims linked to evidence, and conclusions, all structured

What Is a Science Notebook?

by an investigation leading to an understanding of "big ideas," not just factoids in science. As such, a science notebook is a central place where language, data, and experience work together to form meaning for the student. This form of competence or expertise is developed through active construction of knowledge. Students need time and practice using science notebooks to attain expertise.

Student science notebooks, used well, become an embedded element in the curriculum and thus serve as a ready source of recorded data for both the student and the teacher. Notebooks become a direct measure of student understanding of the implemented curriculum and become an important means for formative assessment. The science notebooks also reflect an accounting of the progression of an investigation as students formulate and record questions, make predictions, develop a plan of action, record observations, measurements, and data, link claims to evidence, draw conclusions, and finally reflect on the investigation. They are the students' personal record that can be referred to and revised throughout an investigation or even an entire unit of study. The science notebooks also serve as the evidence used in group and class discussion.

There are many different approaches to having students create and utilize science notebooks: composition books, blank or grid-paged lab books, blank or lined sheets of paper stapled together, or loose-leaf binders.

In primary grades, class or group science notebooks may be created for a unit of study instead of individual student notebooks. Classroom teachers often form covers in the shape of the unit of study such as a round cover if students are studying the planets or the moon. Students as early as kindergarten should be encouraged to keep a record of science investigations. Often these entries will come in the form of scribbles or drawings only decipherable to the student. These form the foundation for later work when more specific criteria and writing prompts or sentence starters are more formally introduced. The main objective is for teachers to initially provide students with the opportunity to record their science investigation. Figure 2.1 is a sample page from a flip chart a third-grade student created during an investigation of brine shrimp.

This sample flip-chart page is an example of a student just starting to use a science notebook. The classroom teacher was focusing on observation and recording data with this investigation. The sample page shows the procedures this child followed in hatching the brine shrimp. It also depicts an understanding of the growth cycle of the brine shrimp with drawings and observations recorded. Finally, the sample page includes a reflection of how the student felt about the investigation.

Scientists keep notebooks; students should do likewise. Scientist's notebooks include what worked and what did not work in the investigation. They sometimes learn much more from what did not work. These notebooks include data, drawings, charts, and reflections, as well as new questions. Scientist entries are a record of what was learned at the time of the investigation and is not crossed out or erased when new discoveries take place. Newer ideas, thoughts, and reflections are added as new entries. Classroom teachers should adjust their teaching to provide students with the opportunity to use science notebooks in much the same way scientists do. The chapters that follow provide teachers with the support necessary to accomplish this task.

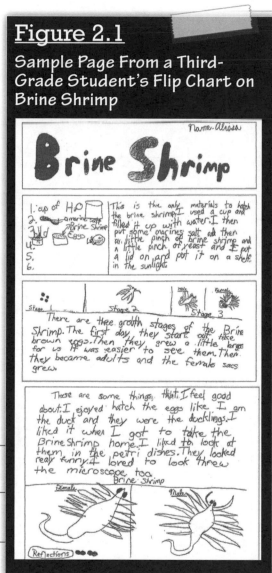

Figure 2.1

Sample Page From a Third-Grade Student's Flip Chart on Brine Shrimp

What Are the Essential Components of a Science Notebook?

S
even research-based science notebook components, and associated criteria for each of these components, have been identified and used by teachers in Imperial County, California, since 1996 (Klentschy and Molina-De La Torre 2004). While these seven components will be found in student science notebook entries associated with most lessons, they are not necessarily found in student science notebook entries for all lessons.

What Are the Essential Components of a Science Notebook?

These seven components are:

- Question, Problem, Purpose

- Prediction

- Developing a Plan

- Observations, Data, Charts, Graphs, Drawings and Illustrations

- Claims and Evidence

- Drawing Conclusions

- Reflection—Next Steps and New Questions

While each of these components can be viewed as individually important to the process of helping students carry out science activities and investigations, they collectively form a framework classroom teachers can use to help students make sense of what they have investigated. Figure 3.1 is an example of a science notebook entry of a fourth-grade student from a unit on magnetism and electricity. All of the components except planning are present in this entry and the student combined the conclusion and reflection.

The Question/Problem/Purpose component is the starting point for any student science investigation. Questions should be student generated, either from an individual, group, or class set of focus questions related to either solving a problem or answering a question that has been raised. Students should write questions in their own words. The questions should also be clear and concise and relate to the objective or standard being investigated. Student questions should also be investigable and not just simply be answered "yes" or "no." In the sample student science notebook entry (Figure 3.1), the student writes a focus question: Which objects stick to magnets? This is an investigable question. Chapter 5 provides strategies to help students formulate appropriate questions.

The Prediction component is designed to have students make a prediction regarding a reason-

Figure 3.1

Fourth-Grade Student's Sample Notebook Entry from Magnetism and Electricity

Sience

Investigation I—The Force

Investigation I - The Force
12/08/04
Focus Question
Which object stick to magnets?

Prediction
I predict the magnet will stick to the metal things because I think the magnet is or metal too.

Will stick	Does not stick
① shiny nails	rubber band ①
② dull nails	craft stick ②
③ pieces of screen	sponge ③
④ paper fasteners	soda straws ④
⑤ paper clips	pieces of yarn ⑤
⑥ screws	black rocks ⑥
⑦ brass rings	river pebbles ⑦
⑧ washers	pieces of cardboard ⑧
	plastic chips ⑨
	aluminum foil ⑩

able answer to the question they formulated. Teachers need to assist students in writing predictions that connect to prior experience and relate to the question they formulated. Predictions should be clear and reasonable. A good prediction also gives an explanation or a reason. Using the word "because" assists students in providing an explanation. In the sample notebook entry, the student uses the word "because" in her prediction, providing an explanation based on prior knowledge. Chapter 6 discusses strategies to assist students in developing effective predictions.

Developing a Plan relates to the student detailing a course of action to obtain data for the investigation. This usually takes place in two stages. First the student develops a general plan where variables and controls are identified and then an operational plan where a clear sequence and direction for the investigation is outlined. The operational plan also includes the materials needed for the investigation. In the sample entry, the teacher had the students develop a class plan and it was recorded on the chalkboard. An important aspect for developing a plan is for students to also create a data collection device for the investigation. In the sample entry, a T-Chart was selected as the data collection device. Strategies for developing plans are explored in Chapter 7.

The Observations, Data, Charts, Graphs, Drawings, and Illustrations component is designed to provide students with strategies to collect data related to their question and plan from observations or measurements during the implementation of their plan. These strategies include student-generated drawings and illustrations, charts, graphs, and an accompanying narrative. In the sample student science notebook entry, the student has created a

Figure 3.1 (Cont.)

Data

Things that stick	This that don't stick
shiny nails	dull nails
black rocks	soda straws
pieces of screen	sponges
paper fasteners	river pebbles
paper clips	pieces of copper
washers	pieces of yarn
screws	pieces of cardboards
	rubber band
	craft sticks
	brass rings
	aluminium foil
	plastic chips

Claims and Evidence   12/13/04

Claims	Evidence
Magnet does not stick to all metal objects	It didn't sticks to the dull nail, brass ring foil and copper
The magnet did not stick to anything not made of metal	It didn't stick to wood paper, yarn, plastc. etc
The magnet stuck to the black rock	I observed it sticking.

12/14/04

① I claim that magnet stuck to the black rock because the evidence shows that I saw it sticking.

② I claim that the magnet did not stick to anything not made of metal because the evidence shows that it didn't stick to wood, paper, plastic, etc.

③ I claim that magnet does not stick to all metal because the evidence shows that it didn't sticks to the dull nail, brass rings, foil, and copper.

① Conclusion / Reflection
My prediction was wrong because the magnet didn't stick to everything that was metal.

I was very amazed that it didn't stick to everything that was metal

I learned that the magnet only stuck to steel things or iron.

What Are the Essential Components of a Science Notebook?

T-Chart with column headings of "Things that stick" and "This [sic] that don't stick" to collect and organize data. Chapter 8 introduces strategies to assist students in effectively collecting, organizing, and displaying their data.

Claims and Evidence is where students use the data they have collected during their investigation to make sense or meaning from the investigation. Students need to understand that their data is their evidence. Students often make many claims in science without supporting them with evidence from their investigation. In the sample entry, the student again is using a T-Chart to record claims and evidence and then rewriting the listings as complete sentences. Chapter 9 provides classroom teachers with several writing supports to assist students in effectively linking claims to evidence.

The Drawing Conclusions component is designed to assist students in recording what they learned from the investigation, not simply what they did during the investigation. While this may seem easy on face value, it is actually quite difficult for many students to do. In the sample notebook entry, the student comes to the conclusion that, "the magnet only stuck to steel things or iron." This was the teacher's content objective for this lesson. The teacher also had the student revisit her prediction and revise her thinking regarding what would "stick" to the magnet. Chapter 10 discusses effective strategies to assist students in drawing conclusions.

After students complete an investigation, teachers should consider providing students the opportunity to reflect on what they learned. The Reflection: Next Steps, New Questions component is for that purpose. In the sample entry, the student comments, "I was very amazed that it didn't stick to everything that was metal." Students should also have the opportunity to extend their investigation with a new application of their original question. Chapter 11 explores strategies to help students become more reflective in both their thinking and in their writing in their science notebooks.

When viewed as a whole, these components provide students with the tools to make greater meaning from their science investigations and to use the science notebook as the communication method to do such. Again, time and practice are essential to achieve this end.

4 Getting Started

Learning how to keep a science notebook is developmental both for students and classroom teachers. Many classroom teachers begin the process of recording information using commercial worksheets that were developed to accompany their designated instructional materials. These worksheets sometimes assist students in organizing their data during an investigation. While worksheets may help students begin to learn the process of organizing a science investigation and keeping a record of their data through charts, most fall short of helping students link claims to their data (evidence) and then make a generalization of what they learned during the investigation (Aschbacher and Baker 2003).

Getting Started

There are a variety of ways classroom teachers can use worksheets as a starting point. Some teachers reproduce them and have students staple or paste them into their science notebooks. Others only use the data collection devices such as charts and tables as a way of modeling the tools for recording data, observations, or measurements.

Students may have difficulty recording items in science notebooks in the early stages. It is important that classroom teachers provide writing prompts or sentence stems to facilitate the process. There are several ways to get started with student science notebooks. Sentence stems such as those listed below can be initially introduced and then gradually removed as students gain experience. These stems introduce students to the essential science notebook components.

My question: _____ (Question)

Today I (or we) want to find out_____ (Problem)

I think _____ will happen because _____ (Prediction)

I noticed (or observed) _____ (Observation)

Today I learned _____ (Conclusion)

I wonder _____ (Reflection)

Questions I have now are _____ (Next Steps/New Questions)

Students should also be encouraged in the early stages of development to record the date and time in their notebooks along with any other important headings or titles for their work. This will add purpose to their work and allow students to return to previous entries to determine how their thinking has changed over time. Students will also be introduced to the notion that the science notebook is their record of what was observed or measured and that this information is available for future use.

For more ideas on stems, visit the Valle Imperial Project in Science website at *www.vipscience.com.* Additional websites such as the East Bay, Rhode Island Collaborative at *www.ebecri.org/custom/toolkit.html* and the North Cascades and Olympic Science Partnership at *www.sciencenotebooks.org* offer resources to help classroom teachers get started using science notebooks.

Students will develop proficiency if classroom teachers give them time and multiple recording experiences. In the early stages of using science notebooks, students may have difficulty deciding how and what to record. Classroom discussion at key junctures in the investigation helps students focus their science notebook entries, provides opportunities for teachers to model suggested formats, and allows teachers to use examples from other students as models.

Just as students develop the ability to use science notebooks over time with practice, teachers also master the use of science notebooks by making them part of their instructional practice. For example, a kindergarten teacher integrated the use of science notebooks in her classroom instruction over a period of time, reaching a comfort level both in her expectations for what students had the ability to do and with her existing beliefs regarding the use of science notebooks in her classroom.

In Figure 4.1, the teacher is using a commercially developed worksheet and has traced the letter shapes for her students. While this is not the most effective practice, because the ownership for the work belongs to the teacher, it still represents a recognition that having her students record information from their science investigation will increase their understanding of what they were supposed to learn.

The second stage of this teacher's development is depicted in Figure 4.2. The teacher has given the student a blank sheet of paper and the student has drawn his observation of the relationship between the Sun, himself, and his shadow. The student has dictated a title for his observation and the teacher has recorded the title. It is evident from the drawing that two important pieces of information are being noted by the student: (1) he activated prior knowledge in drawing his likeness (the previous unit of study was

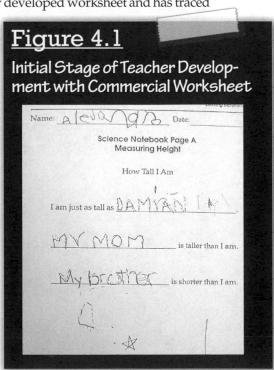

Figure 4.1

Initial Stage of Teacher Development with Commercial Worksheet

Name: Alexandra   Date:

Science Notebook Page A
Measuring Height

How Tall I Am

I am just as tall as DAMIAN I M

MY MOM _____ is taller than I am.

My brother _____ is shorter than I am.

Getting Started

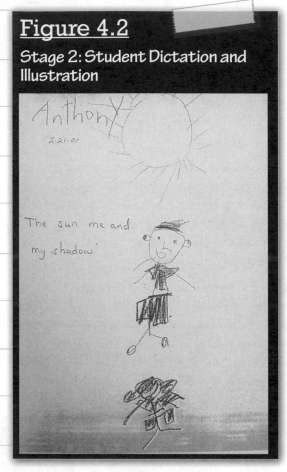

Figure 4.2
Stage 2: Student Dictation and Illustration

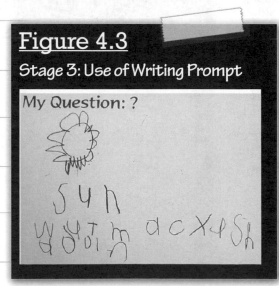

Figure 4.3
Stage 3: Use of Writing Prompt

Myself and Others); and (2) the student has a misconception in the alignment of where his shadow belongs. Using this information, the teacher can work with the student to clarify this misconception before proceeding. The task of just tracing letters on a commercial worksheet would not have revealed this misconception.

The teacher gave the students writing prompts and sentence starters to record and illustrate their observations. In Figure 4.3, the student has responded to the writing prompt of "My Question" by drawing and labeling the Sun and then recording a question: What makes a shadow? This question was student-generated from a class discussion about shadows after the teacher had read a story about shadows to the students.

Another example of this stage is depicted in Figure 4.4, where the teacher again provides a sentence starter for the student: "Today I learned…."

The student responded to the sentence starter by drawing a picture of a flashlight, an object, and the resulting shadow created by shining the flashlight on the object. The student has also recorded that he learned that the "[shadow is] opposite the light."

Both of these examples provide a cognitive map of what students observed and their thoughts of the observation. This process was facilitated by the teacher through the use of sentence starters or writing prompts. The students demonstrated a good understanding of the primary focus of the lesson in both the formulation of a question and in recording what they had learned.

Figure 4.5 illustrates the final stage of this teacher's development in the integration of science notebooks into her science instruction.

In this stage, the teacher gave the students paper with a large blank space on top for illustrating observations and lines on the bottom for recording findings. This student is writing a prediction regarding the number of paper clips she thinks will be needed to sink the piece of plywood floating in a small tub of water. The student wrote: " Prediction—I wil (sic) need 5 clips to sico (sic) the wood." After conducting the investigation, the student recorded: " I iyou (sic) 3 clips."

In this stage the student has taken control and is making her own meaning from the investigation. The teacher has the role of facilitator, providing the prompts or supports to help the student become more experienced in the use of science notebooks.

In summary, the process of using science notebooks is developmental for both students and classroom teachers. Student supports through commercial worksheets, writing prompts, and sentence starters are effective ways for students to begin using science notebooks to make sense from their science investigations. Integration of these strategies into classroom science curriculum is also a key element in this developmental process.

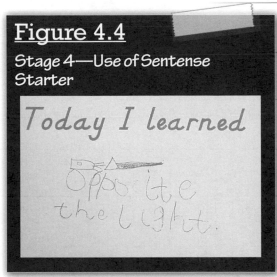

Figure 4.4

Stage 4—Use of Sentense Starter

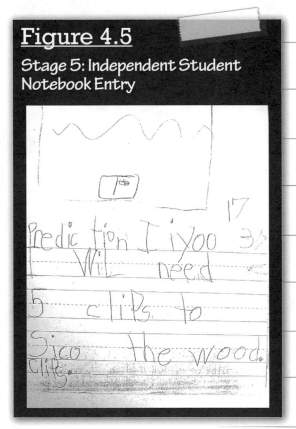

Figure 4.5

Stage 5: Independent Student Notebook Entry

CHAPTER 5

Question, Problem, Purpose

Scientists begin an investigation with a question or a problem to solve. In elementary science, students also raise different types of questions, procedural and investigative. Many times students just want to find out the "how" or the "what" of something. Every classroom science investigation usually begins with students asking themselves one of the following questions:

What do I want to find out?

What is the reason for my question?

What problem am I addressing?

Questions and question-formulating strategies are central to science. In many ways the formulation of a question forms the basis for high-quality instruction in science. Effective questioning has a strong connection to cognitive

Question, Problem, Purpose

theory. In an era of standards, assessment, and accountability, where a specific set of science concepts are assigned to a grade level, most of the question-formulation strategies classroom teachers will need to consider will be having students create and test investigable questions.

Classroom science investigations usually begin with students being posed with a problem or situation to resolve. From this problem or situation, the teacher guides the students with the following prompts:

What is our problem?

What do we want to know or find out?

Teachers should then have students work in small groups to define the problem or to define what they want to find out. The small group discussion then evolves into a class discussion, with each group sharing their interpretation of the problem or what they want to find out, while the teacher lists the questions on a chart or on the chalkboard.

In one third-grade classroom, the teacher started this process by reading the following engaging scenario to the class:

> *My neighbor, Max, stopped by to show me a set of minerals he inherited from his grandfather. He told me that these were minerals and not rocks. Max said that minerals are usually of one color and rocks have many colors because rocks are made of more than one mineral. He wants to identify the minerals using some old charts and tools he found in the box. Max's dad is a rock collector and wants him to classify the minerals using the available material. Max needs to identify the minerals first, in order to later identify which minerals are found in his dad's rock collection. I brought some samples of the minerals, charts and tools so we can help him. What is the problem for this investigation?*

The teacher then asked each group of students to discuss the scenario and to write a focus question for what they thought they needed to find out in order to solve the problem. The teacher then listed each group's focus question on the board because the class was just starting to use science notebooks. The teacher used this class set of focus questions to start a discussion about writing focus questions. Figure 5.1 is the class set of focus questions.

The teacher then asked the students to consider which of the questions related to the problem they were trying to solve. The class decided that the problem to solve was "Identify the minerals using the charts and tools," and that none of the questions addressed this problem. The teacher then prompted the students to turn the problem into a question. The class created the following question: How can we identify the minerals using the charts and tools?

In the early stages of using science notebooks and formulating focus questions, students will also often ask questions that can be answered "yes" or "no." Teachers should work with students to rephrase these types of questions to make them more open-ended. Figure 5.2 is another example of a student science notebook entry from a fifth-grade class just starting to use science notebooks. Note that the class focus question can be answered "yes" or "no."

The classroom teacher then initiated a discussion of the class set of focus questions, guiding students to rephrase their questions to kinds that could not be answered "yes" or "no." The students soon learned that *how, what,* and *which* were good words to use in writing focus questions. After some additional class discussion, the class rephrased the question to: How will the properties of the sample elements of _____ change when placed in a warm container?

The class discussion then shifted back to the small groups, where they rewrote their focus questions. The teacher worked with each group to help model questions that are investigable. Some guiding questions that the teacher used to prompt the discussion included:

What are we trying to find out?

What information do we expect to obtain?

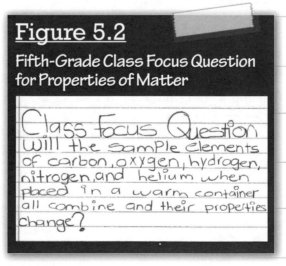

Figure 5.1

Third-Grade Class Focus Questions for Rocks and Minerals

Group Focus Questions:
1) Why did the neighbor want to identify his rocks and minerals? (Daylene, Elba)

2) How many minerals does it take to make a rock? (Gabriel, Isiah)

3) What is the difference between rocks and minerals? (Roc, Neil, Eddie)

4) How much time does it take to form a rock and a mineral? (Melanie, Tatiana)

5) How is this unit relate to our science unit? (Christian, Denny)

6) What is the difference in the size of a rock and a mineral? (Tyler, Jesse)

Figure 5.2

Fifth-Grade Class Focus Question for Properties of Matter

Class Focus Question
Will the sample elements of carbon, oxygen, hydrogen, nitrogen, and helium when placed in a warm container all combine and their properties change?

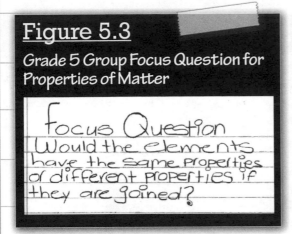

Figure 5.3

Grade 5 Group Focus Question for Properties of Matter

> Focus Question
> Would the elements have the same properties or different properties if they are joined?

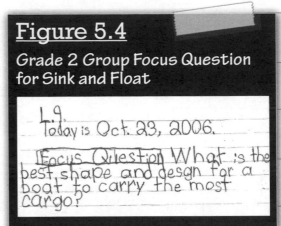

Figure 5.4

Grade 2 Group Focus Question for Sink and Float

> L.9.
> Today is Oct. 23, 2006.
> Focus Question What is the best shape and design for a boat to carry the most cargo?

In another fifth-grade classroom, a group of students wrote the focus question displayed in Figure 5.3. The classroom teacher guided the group using the prompt, "What are we trying to find out?" to rephrase their focus question to: What will happen to the properties of the elements if they are joined together?

The formulation of an investigable focus question is based on the cognitive development of students. Kindergarten students are developmentally capable of formulating what, when, and how questions. First- and second-grade students have the ability to convert questions of wondering into investigable questions. Students in grades 3–6 are capable of formulating simple and complex investigable questions. The development of investigable questions leads to the development of scientific reasoning. Figure 5.4 is an example of an investigable question formulated by a group of second-grade students. This is an investigable question because it addressed the design problem of the best shape for a clay boat. The students could test a variety of shapes and designs to determine which clay boat could carry the most cargo (paper clips).

Investigable questions are questions that are not usually answered with a simple yes or no. Why questions are very difficult for elementary students to investigate. Teachers should encourage students to convert both of these types of questions into how, what, or which questions. These types of questions are more appropriate for elementary students to base their classroom science experiences around. There are many different categories of investigable questions. The context of the investigation will usually determine the category of question most appropriate for the investigation. Figure 5.5 is an example of an investigable question formulated by a third-grade student studying brine shrimp.

This is an investigable question because it addresses the problem that the students were presented with—an unknown white substance was found on sheets of black paper on their desks. The problem was to determine the nature of the substance.

Classroom teachers typically start with their students using a question from the commercial science program and then shift to student-generated questions as students become more familiar with investigative science. Using the commercial worksheet focus questions will also provide students with models to help them formulate their own questions. Recording questions in their science notebooks is important, as this will become a permanent record that students can refer to at later stages in the investigation.

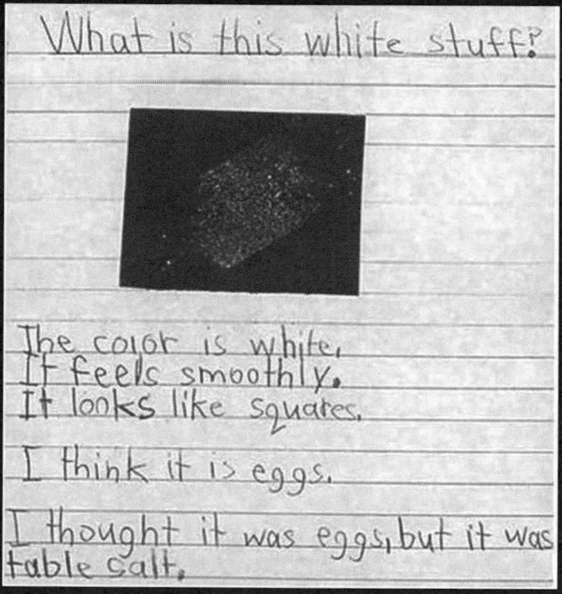

As stated, the category of student-generated focus questions usually is determined by the context of the investigation. If the context of the investigation requires measuring and counting, students will typically write measuring and counting questions. If the context of the investigation requires comparisons, students will then typically write comparison questions. Students will also just write problem-posing focus questions based on the "how" and "what" of the phenomena that they are investigating.

Measuring and counting questions help students move from a qualitative to a quantitative observation in their investigation. Examples of measuring and counting types of question prompts that teachers may consider using with students include:

> **How many...?**
>
> **How long...?**
>
> **How often...?**

Comparison questions help students order their observations and data. They again are quantitative questions, and question-starting prompts that teachers may consider include:

> **How much longer is _____ than _____?**
>
> **How much shorter is _____ than_____?**
>
> **How are_____ and _____ the same?**

Figure 5.5

Grade 3 Student Focus Question for Brine Shrimp

What is this white stuff?

The color is white,
It feels smoothly,
It looks like squares,

I think it is eggs,

I thought it was eggs, but it was table salt,

Question, Problem, Purpose

How are _____ and _____ different?

Or

Which object is the heaviest?

Which object is the lightest?

Which object has the highest pitch?

These starting prompts can gradually be removed as students gain practice in formulating their own focus questions.

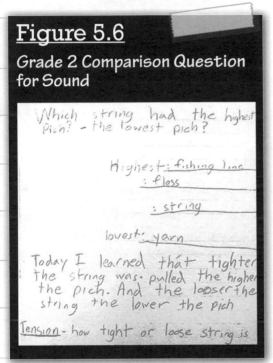

Figure 5.6

Grade 2 Comparison Question for Sound

> Which string had the highest Pich? - the lowest pich?
>
> Highest: fishing line
> : floss
>
> : string
>
> lowest: yarn
>
> Today I learned that tighter the string was pulled the higher the pich. And the looser the string the lower the pich
>
> Tension - how tight or loose string is

Figure 5.7

Grade 3 Comparison Question for Rocks and Minerals

> Sept. 13, 2006
>
> Class Focus Question:
> 1. How are rocks different from minerals?
>
> Prediction:
> I think minerals are sometimes sharpe and sometimes smooth.

Students need to be guided to frame only questions that are investigable. Again, questions that can be answered "yes" or "no" should be avoided. The best questions for elementary student investigations usually start with "how" or "what." When the science investigation is linked to resolve a real-world problem, students usually frame richer questions.

Figure 5.6 provides an example of a second-grade student's science notebook entry asking a comparison question: Which has the highest pitch? The lowest pitch? This is an example of an investigable question. The student can design an investigation to compare the pitch (high to low) from a variety of materials as well as the tightness of the material.

Figure 5.7 is an example of a comparison question formulated by a third-grade student regarding the differences between rocks and minerals.

This is a good example of an investigable comparison question because the student can design an investigation to compare the similarities and differences between rocks and minerals.

Figure 5.8 is an example of a comparison question formulated by a group of fifth-grade students examining the differences between the transportation systems of plants and humans.

This is a good comparison question because it focuses the student's investigation. Note that the prediction shows some misconceptions regarding transportation systems in plants and animals.

Classroom teachers can guide students to create other types of investigable focus questions. These types address students' need to learn more about phenomena in the real world:

What would happen if _____?

What does_____?

How does____ affect the____?

Figure 5.8
Grade 5 Comparison Question for Human Body Systems

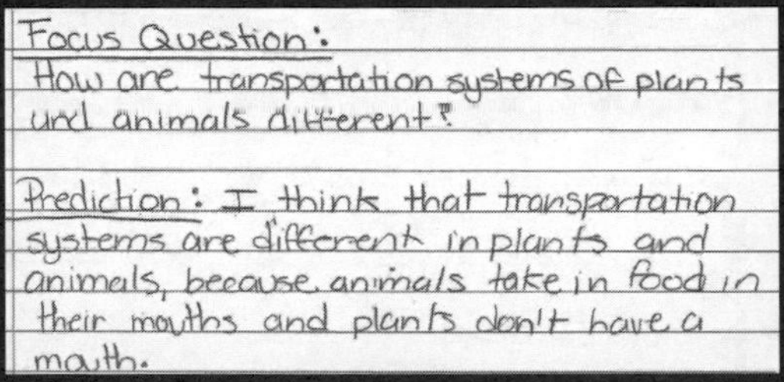

Focus Question:
How are transportation systems of plants and animals different?

Prediction: I thinks that transportation systems are different in plants and animals, because animals take in food in their mouths and plants don't have a mouth.

Figure 5.9
Grade 4 Focus Question for Magnetism and Electricity

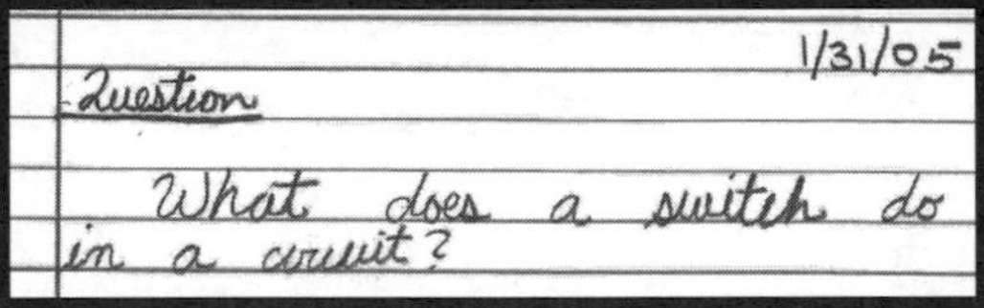

1/31/05
Question
What does a switch do in a circuit?

Figure 5.9 is an example of a focus question from a group of fourth-grade students wondering what function a switch performs in a circuit.

These types of questions lend themselves to investigation and also help students to formulate predictions by accessing their prior knowledge. They also prompt students to explore the properties of unfamiliar materials.

Examples of sentence starters for problem-posing questions include:

What happens to____ if we change ____?

How do we_____?

How can we_____?

Figure 5.10 is a good example of a problem-posing question created by a group of fourth-grade students in their study of magnetism and electricity. The teacher gave the students the scenario that they were at Disney World on the Haunted Mansion ride and the power went out. They searched through their backpacks and found a wire, a battery, and a bulb. Someone in the group remembered that these items could be connected to make a light, but forgot how. The question in Figure 5.10 addresses

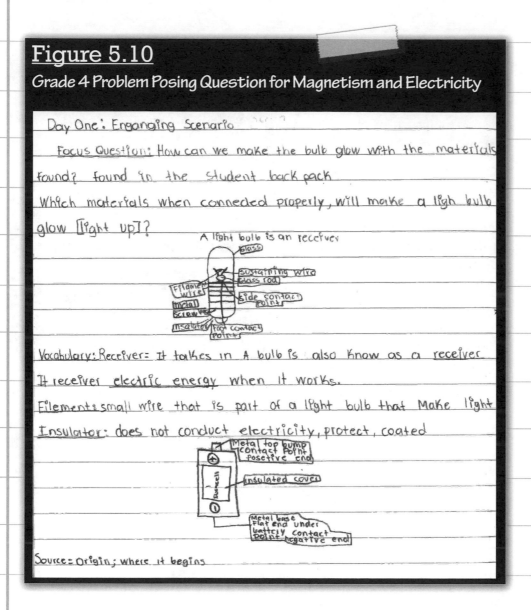

Figure 5.10

Grade 4 Problem Posing Question for Magnetism and Electricity

Day One: Engaging Scenario

Focus Question: How can we make the bulb glow with the materials found? found in the student back pack

Which materials when connected properly, will make a ligh bulb glow [light up]?

A light bulb is an receiver

Vocabulary: Receiver= It takes in A bulb is also know as a receiver It receiver electric energy when it works.

Filement: small wire that is part of a light bulb that Make light

Insulator: does not conduct electricity, protect, coated

Source= Origin; where it begins

the problem, and as a "how" question, it will assist the students in the design of an investigation to find a solution.

Another good example of a problem-posing question is shown in Figure 5.11. Fifth-grade students formulated a problem-posing question to investigate how to remove the salt from a saline solution.

In summary, investigative science begins with a question. Classroom discussion addressing "What is the problem that needs resolution?" or "What do I want to find out?" helps students write these types of investigable questions. The sentence starters and writing prompts in this chapter have proven to be an effective strategy

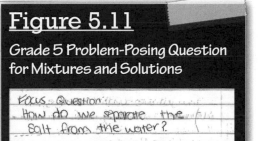

Figure 5.11

Grade 5 Problem-Posing Question for Mixtures and Solutions

Focus Question:
How do we separate the salt from the water?

for teachers in getting students writing investigable questions. After students develop a pattern in their writing, these sentence starters and writing prompts can be removed. Then, through classroom discussion at the beginning of the investigation, the teacher can remind students of the different ways that have been learned to formulate questions.

6 Prediction

Many classroom teachers wonder if they should ask students to state a hypothesis or a prediction when they teach investigative science. For the purpose of this book there is a clear distinction between these two choices. A hypothesis should be considered as a statement based on an analysis of data or events that have occurred in the past. An example of a hypothesis could be an examination of past weather patterns with an analysis of temperature changes

Prediction

over a period of time and the factors that may have contributed to such (e.g., a scientist making a hypothesis regarding global warming). A prediction on the other hand, is a statement about something that will occur in the future. An example of a prediction is a statement attempting to explain what will happen when a battery, a wire, and a bulb are configured in a certain way to produce light based on the individual's prior knowledge.

In classroom practice, a prediction then is actually a conditional statement made by the student focusing on what they think will happen as a result of conducting the investigation. Students must be guided to state not only what they think will happen, but also a reason or explanation for what will happen based upon their prior knowledge. Activating student prior knowledge is one of the three major recommendations made by the National Research Council (2005) for classroom teachers to consider in planning effective classroom instruction. Activating prior knowledge provides the student with a gateway or bridge to link the "strange new" with the "familiar old." Therefore, prediction is really more than just an "educated guess." Classroom teachers can use sentence starters and writing prompts to assist students in crafting predictions. Predicting what will happen in the investigation is also similar to the reading comprehension strategy of predicting what will happen next in a story that is being read. Predictions will often provide the teacher with insight into student thinking, prior knowledge, and existing misconceptions.

There are several ways that teachers can assist students in making and writing predictions. One effective practice is for students to draw a diagram, picture, or illustration of what they think will happen along with a brief written explanation. Another effective practice is to use a prompt or sentence starter. When students start writing predictions, classroom teachers can consider using sentence starters such as:

> I think _____ will happen because...

or

> If _____ then _____ because...

The prediction must also relate to the focus question formulated by the student to start the investigation. The use of the word "because" in the prompt or sentence starter calls for an explanation or reason derived from prior knowledge and becomes a statement of what the student currently knows or does not know related to the science content of the investigation.

Younger students or students with limited English speaking abilities usually start making predictions by making a drawing or illustration of their prediction. Figure 6.1 is an example of a kindergarten student's prediction of what he or she thought would happen in an investigation with balls and ramps. In the drawing, the student predicts that each time a ramp is elevated by one stacking cube, the ball will roll farther. This is a reasonable prediction based on the student's prior knowledge that the angle of a ramp is influenced by its height and will cause a ball to roll a greater distance when released from the top of the ramp.

Figure 6.2 is an example of a prediction made by a second-grade student prior to conducting an investigation on sink and float. The teacher has used the sentence starter "I think _____ because…" with the class to help them write predictions. Notice how student prior knowledge related to size and weight of objects has been activated by using "because" and is used as an explanation of what the student thinks will sink and what will float.

As a comparison, Figure 6.3 (p. 34) is an example of a prediction made by a second-grade student in another classroom where the teacher only asked the student to predict what they think will happen in the investigation of how much cargo (gram mass pieces) a clay boat will hold. The teacher did not use a sentence starter with "because" to activate prior knowledge or to ask the student for an explanation for their prediction. The student has used gram mass pieces in previous lessons, but there is no stated reason or explanation made by the student. The prediction may relate to the focus question, but does not provide the classroom teacher with any insight into student thinking or misconceptions.

In Chapter 5, a group of fifth-grade students developed a focus question comparing the transportation systems of plants and humans. Figure 6.4 (p. 34) is an example of the prediction a student formulated that related to the focus question, activated prior knowledge by using "because," and included

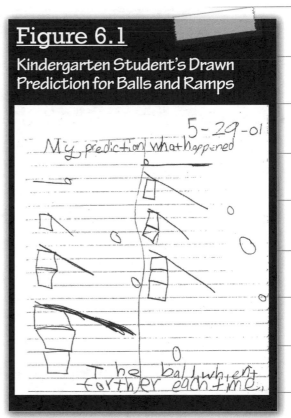

Figure 6.1
Kindergarten Student's Drawn Prediction for Balls and Ramps

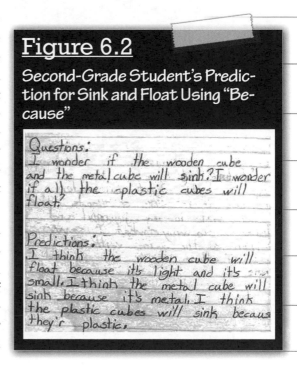

Figure 6.2
Second-Grade Student's Prediction for Sink and Float Using "Because"

Figure 6.3

Contrasting Second-Grade Student's Prediction for Sink and Float Not Using "Because"

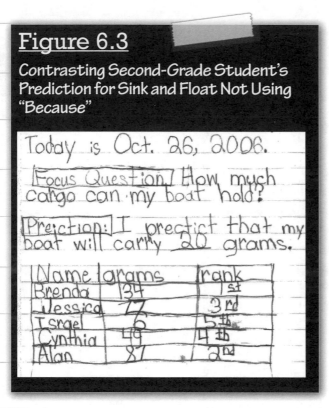

Today is Oct. 26, 2006.

[Focus Question] How much cargo can my boat hold?

[Prediction:] I predict that my boat will carry 20 grams.

Name	grams	rank
Brenda	134	1st
Jessica	7	3rd
Israel	6	5th
Cynthia	49	4th
Alan	87	2nd

Figure 6.4

Fifth Grade Prediction Meeting Criteria for Predictions

Focus Question:
How are transportation systems of plants and animals different?

Prediction: I think that transportation systems are different in plants and animals, because animals take in food in their mouths and plants don't have a mouth.

an explanation or reason. The prediction demonstrates that the student has a naïve understanding and possible misconceptions regarding the similarities and differences between the transportation systems of plants and animals. This information gave the teacher an insight into current student thinking with regard to this concept and became a valuable tool for future lesson planning.

Figure 6.5 is an example of how student predictions written using "because" can provide the teacher with insight into student misconceptions. A group of fifth-grade students formulated an investigation question to determine if an amount of salt (compound) were added to a beaker of water, would the resulting solute be heavier than just the salt and water alone. Their prediction indicated that there was a misconception regarding the difference between a solute, compound, and a mixture. Later, the teacher asked the students to provide examples of a solute (Kool-Aid), a compound (sugar), and a mixture (trail mix). This helped the students describe what they measured and the manner in which they reported their claims, evidence, and conclusions.

In Figure 6.6, a fourth-grade student predicted that if more magnets are added to a magnet cluster, a stronger magnet would be created that would be able to attract more washers. The student had prior knowledge that a larger magnet had greater strength than a smaller magnet and explained that magnets joined together would progressively have more strength than just a single magnet.

In summary, the predictions students write should activate prior knowledge, relate to their focus questions, be conditional statements, and provide an explanation or reason.

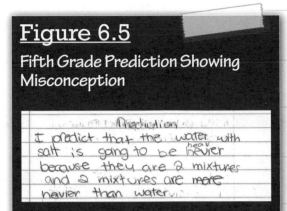

Figure 6.5
Fifth Grade Prediction Showing Misconception

Prediction
I predict that the water with salt is going to be hevier because they are 2 mixtures and 2 mixtures are more havier than water.

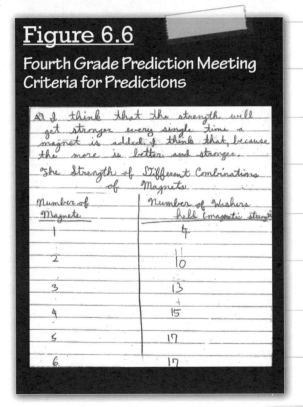

Figure 6.6
Fourth Grade Prediction Meeting Criteria for Predictions

I think that the strength will get stronger every single time a magnet is added. I think that, because the more is better and stronger.

The Strength of Different Combinations of Magnets

Number of Magnets	Number of Washers held (magnetic strength)
1	4
2	10
3	13
4	15
5	17
6	17

7 Planning

Planning or creating a plan of action establishes the steps students will follow to seek an answer to their focus question or resolve their problem through "testing" their prediction. Planning criteria relate to how the investigation will be conducted. There are some common elements classroom teachers should use to assist their students in creating a plan. The plan should relate to the investigable question, sequence, materials, and a data organizer. The plan should also identify the materials that will be used in the investigation. Many teachers also believe that in order for a plan to be effective, it should be written in a manner that the student or someone else could follow it and replicate the results of the investigation. Replication is

Planning

an important concept for elementary students to understand because it is related to the nature of investigative science. Replication of an investigation provides students with a basis to determine if their results were "one time" or something that one could expect to occur each time the investigation was conducted.

When students have little or no experience either with the science content or the context of the focus of the investigation, planning can be a difficult process. Mastering the skill of planning is a "learn by doing" process. Teachers can use a variety of writing prompts and supports to assist students in learning how to plan.

Teachers can teach students how to plan by scaffolding the process. These writing prompts or scaffolds are initially supplied by the teacher and are gradually removed as students become proficient in the planning process. Teachers already use writing prompts and sentence starters to assist students in writing investigable questions and predictions, and investigable questions and predictions lay the foundation for the development of plans.

Planning scaffolds can be used to assist students in two stages of the planning process: Stage 1—developing a general plan; and Stage 2—developing an operational plan of action.

The writing prompts used in the first stage—developing a general plan—assist the students in identifying and determining "what will be changed" (the independent variable); "what will stay the same" (the control variables); and "the outcome to observe or measure" (the dependent variable). These are the three factors that students need to understand are the elements of conducting a "fair test." A fair test is one where only one thing (variable) is changed for the investigation. This will help students to determine how changing just the one variable influences the outcome of the investigation. Once this generalized plan has been established, the second stage of planning—the development of the operational plan—can take form. The operational plan is the sequence of procedures, events, or steps that will be taken by the student during the investigation.

A class of students was conducting fair tests with Wisconsin Fast Plants. One group of students developed the following focus question:

How does the amount of fertilizer affect plant growth?

Their classroom teacher provided the students with the following planning chart to use to create their general plan:

Planning Step	General Plan
1. What should be changed?	
2. What should be kept the same?	
3. How will differences be observed or measured?	

This type of general planning chart directs the students back to their focus question (How does the amount of fertilizer affect plant growth?) and prompts them to plan a fair test. The students used this planning chart to devise the following General Plan:

Planning Step	General Plan
1. What should be changed?	1. The amount of fertilizer in each planting quad.
2. What should be kept the same?	2. The amount of water. The amount of light. The amount of soil. The same temperature.
3. How will differences be observed or measured?	3. The height of the plant. The number of seeds in each pod.

After discussing this general plan with the students, the teacher added a third column to their planning chart. The students were then asked to write the specific steps they would follow. The resulting operational plan is below:

Planning Step	General Plan	Operational Plan (Steps to follow)
1. What should be changed?	1. The amount of fertilizer in each planting quad.	1. Add 1, 3, 5 drops of fertilizer t three different planting quads. Label the quads.
2. What should be kept the same?	2. The amount of water. The amount of light. The amount of soil. The same temperature.	2. Measure and give equal amounts of water to each quad. Use a thermometer to measure temperature for each quad. Use equal amounts of light from the light stand. Use equal amounts of soil.
3. How will differences be observed or measured?	3. The height of the plant. The number of seeds in each pod.	3. Measure height of plant each day and record the data. Count the number of seeds from each plant.

Planning

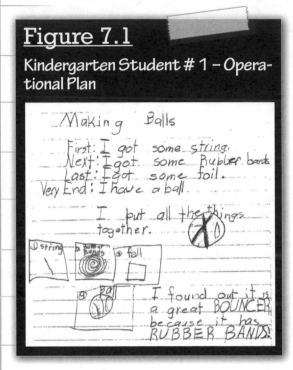

Figure 7.1

Kindergarten Student # 1 – Operational Plan

After a discussion with the students regarding their operational plan, the teacher asked them to write out their operational plan in paragraph form to practice making the series of steps sequential using the following writing prompts:

> **First...**
>
> **Second...**
>
> **Third...**
>
> **Next....**
>
> **Then...**
>
> **Finally...**

These transition words assist students in listing the series of steps and procedures that they will follow in their investigation.

Figures 7.1, 7.2, and 7.3 are examples of how three kindergarten students developed operational plans for making a ball. It is important to note that while all three kindergarten students used the same writing prompt to formulate their operational plan, each was written in the "voice" of the student. The opportunity for students to develop "voice" in their personal science notebooks is very important in helping students understand the science content.

In another classroom, a group of fourth-grade students were investigating electromagnets and wrote this focus question:

How does the number of coils of wire around the bolt affect the strength of the electromagnet?

After discussing the focus question, the teacher gave the students a planning chart:

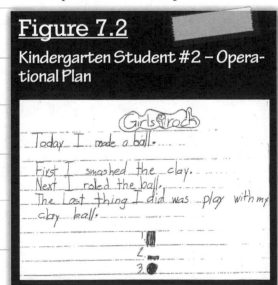

Figure 7.2

Kindergarten Student #2 – Operational Plan

Planning Step	General Plan	Operational Plan
1. What will change?	1.	1.
2. What will stay the same?	2.	2.
3. What will you observe or measure?	3.	3.

The students then devised the general and operational plans for their investigation:

Planning Step	General Plan	Operational Plan
1. What will change?	1. The number of coils around the bolt.	1. Wrap 5, 10, and 20 coils around the bolt.
2. What will stay the same?	2. The size of the bolt The wire The battery Paper clips	2. Use a 6" bolt each time. Use the same amount and type of wire each time. Use the same size battery. Use the same size paper clips each time.
3. What will you observe or measure?	3. The number of paper clips each electromagnet attracts.	3. Record the number of paper clips each electromagnet attracts.

Note that there are differences between the general and operational plans. The general plan identifies what will change (the number of coils of wire around the bolt), what will stay the same (the other materials), and what will be measured (the number of paper clips each electromagnet will attract). In the operational plan, students are developing the outline for the procedures or steps that they will follow in conducting their investigation.

Figure 7.4 is an example of an operational plan developed by a sixth-grade student in an investigation to plan a fair test using Brassica plants. While some of the desired elements are not

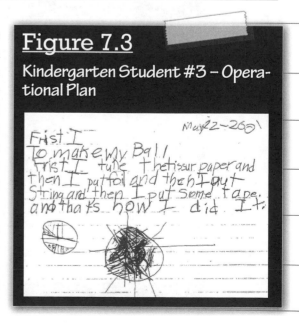

Figure 7.3
Kindergarten Student #3 – Operational Plan

May 22–2001

Frist I
To make my Ball
Frist I tune thetissur paper and
then I put foil and then I put
String and then I put some tape.
and that's how I did It.

Figure 7.4

Sixth-Grade Student's Operational Plan for Conducting a Fair Test

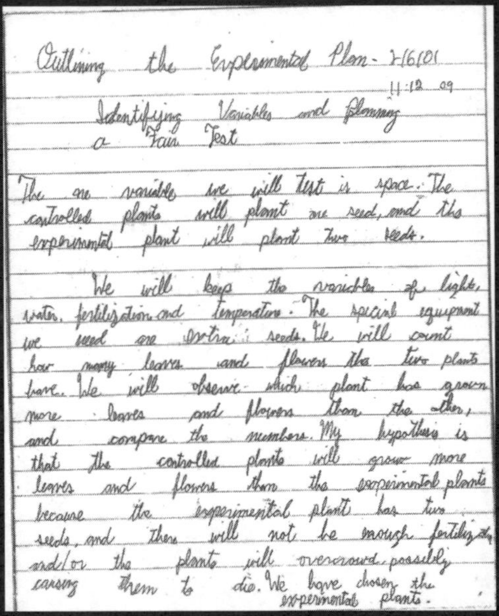

included in the operational plan, this student is demonstrating developmental progress in thinking through what must be changed, what will be kept the same, and what will be observed or measured.

Another example of an operational plan is depicted in Figure 7.5. This fifth-grade student is investigating how to change one variable in a water clock's components (funnel, bead, or washers) that will result in the water clock sinking to the bottom of a tub in 30 seconds instead of 15 seconds. The student has kept the size of the funnel and the number of washers used for weight the same and has changed the size of the bead placed in the bottom of the funnel from 4 mm to 3 mm. The student then describes the procedures that will be followed to conduct the investigation.

Figure 7.5

Fifth-Grade Student's Operational Plan for Sinking Water Clocks

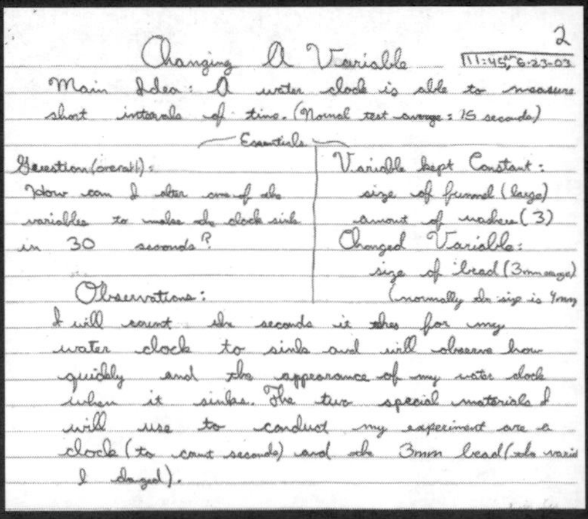

This student is progressing in the development of thinking through what she wants to find out (how to make the clock sink in 30 seconds) and how she is going to conduct the investigation (planning steps). The teacher did not provide a scaffold or prompt for the student to use in developing general and operational plans. The student is clear in what she is going to change and keep the same, but not totally clear in how to perform the procedures for the investigation. Again, scaffolds for planning along with time and practice could greatly assist this student.

The operational plan in Figure 7.6 was written by a fifth-grade student studying pendulums. The student lists the materials that will be used to construct the pendulum, describes the procedures that will be followed for the construction, and draws a diagram to illustrate the finished product. The pendulum was later used in an investigation to determine if the length of the string, the angle of release, or the mass of the bob at the end of the pendulum influenced the number of cycles in 30 seconds.

Figure 7.6

Fifth-Grade Student's Operational Plan for Constructing a Pendulum

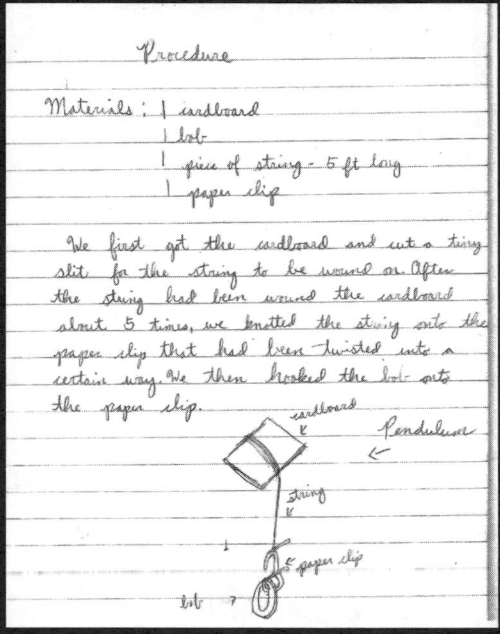
Procedure

Materials: 1 cardboard
1 bob
1 piece of string - 5 ft long
1 paper clip

We first got the cardboard and cut a tiny slit for the string to be wound on. After the string had been wound the cardboard about 5 times, we knotted the string onto the paper clip that had been twisted into a certain way. We then hooked the bob onto the paper clip.

Now that the students have created the "what" of the investigation (the general plan) and the "how" of the investigation (the operational plan), the students will need to determine how they will collect their data, measurements, and observations, which is their evidence. The data organizer is the device the students will create to collect their evidence.

The data organizer may be one of the most difficult aspects of the plan for the students to create. After students create general and operational plans, teachers may ask students one of the following questions:

How will you collect your data?

or

What will you use to collect your data?

Either of these two questions will direct students back to their general and operational plans to re-examine what they are going to observe or measure and how their data will be recorded. There are many ways that data may be collected and recorded. Creating a data collection device can be conducted as a small-group or whole-class activity. Students should be challenged with the aforementioned questions and then be asked to work in their groups to create the data collection device. Each group should share their data collection device with the rest of the class and describe how and why their device will work. Groups can then either use the one they created or one from another group, if their focus questions are similar. Common data collection

Planning

devices are t-tables and charts. Students should be encouraged to label the parts of their chart based upon their operational plan—what they are going to observe or measure. These t-tables or charts can be used to create graphs and other visual representations of the data later in the investigation.

Altering the variable of amount of fertilizer, a sixth-grade group created the following data collection chart:

Comparing the Growth of Plants

Day	1	2	3	4	5	10	11	12	13	14	15	20	25	30	Total number of seeds produced by plant pods
1 drop															
3 drops															
5 drops															

Plant height in centimeters

This chart will be used to collect data related the height of the plants fertilized with one, three, and five drops of fertilizer at different days during the growth cycle of the plant and then to record the number of seeds produced by the different plant pods. This data chart relates back to their general and operational plans.

A fourth-grade group investigating the relationship between the number of coils of current-carrying wire wrapped around an iron bolt and the ability of the electromagnet to pick up paper clips created this data-collection device:

The Strength of an Electromagnet

# of Coils	# of Paper Clips Picked Up
5	
10	
20	

After a class discussion, the group decided to modify their t-table and to conduct three trials with each number of coils to see if the electromagnet would pick up the same number of paper clips with each of the three trials and the same number of coils. Their revised chart looked like this:

The Strength of an Electromagnet

# of Coils	Trial 1	Trial 2	Trial 3	Average
5				
10				
20				

This data collection chart related back to their focus question, prediction, general plan, and operational plan.

Teachers are aware that planning is a developmental process. There needs to be a combination of planning and doing. Students need to try out their plans and then through class discussion, identify the limitations in their operational plans.

Class discussions allow students to share the types of data organizers they have created, providing peer examples to students having difficulty. After the class discussion, the teacher may offer a class data organizer to help students and to serve as a basis for discussion during the "making meaning" conference later in the investigation. Teachers should also be aware not to place too much of a burden on students and allow them to spend too much time in the creation of their plan. Young students will tend to list everything and will consume most of their investigation time just listing materials.

Figure 7.7 is an example of a plan created by a fifth-grade student conducting an investigation with pendulums. The student has developed a data organizer to record the number of cycles made by the pendulum in a 30-second period. Note that the student has identified that more than one trial is necessary to obtain an accurate idea of how adding more mass to the pendulum will impact the number of cycles. The student also gave the data organizer a title and labeled each column to describe the type of data being collected.

Figure 7.7

Fifth-Grade Student's Data Table

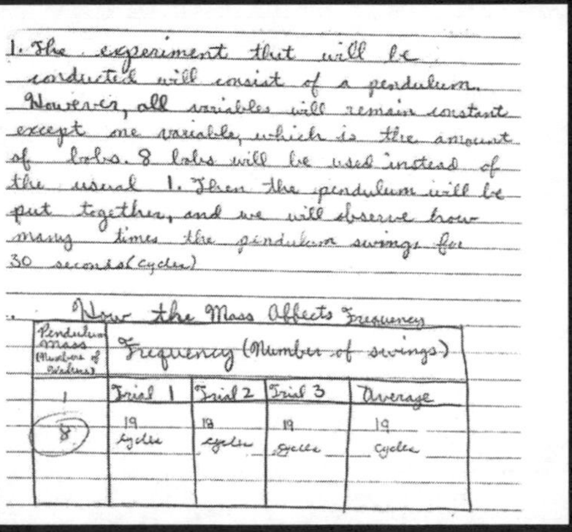

1. The experiment that will be conducted will consist of a pendulum. However, all variables will remain constant except one variable, which is the amount of bobs. 8 bobs will be used instead of the usual 1. Then the pendulum will be put together, and we will observe how many times the pendulum swings for 30 seconds (cycles)

How the Mass Affects Frequency

Pendulum Mass (Numbers of Washers)	Frequency (Number of swings)			
1	Trial 1	Trial 2	Trial 3	Average
8	19 cycles	18 cycles	19 cycles	19 cycles

Learning how to plan a science investigation is an important component of learning how to do investigative science. The plan will guide the students to find evidence to respond to their focus question

Planning

or problem that needs to be solved. When they can (1) use specific criteria in formulating a plan for their investigation; (2) create a general plan outlining what will be changed, kept the same, and observed or measured; (3) devise an operational plan outlining the sequence of events or procedures and materials used in the investigation; and (4) develop a data organizer designed to collect what will be observed or measured, students will be able to perform effective investigations.

CHAPTER 8

Observations, Data, Charts, Graphs, Drawings, and Illustrations

Observation is an important tool for scientists performing investigative science. Observation is also a very important skill for students to learn and use in elementary science. With this skill students use all of their senses as they conduct their investigation. From observations students collect data (their evidence), make drawings and illustrations, make charts and graphs from their data, and comment on what they have observed. These observations are then used to examine and analyze patterns and relationships. Teachers recognize that the skill of observation is developmental and needs to be taught.

Observations, Data, Charts, Graphs, Drawings, and Illustrations

Observation can involve the use of any of the five senses either singularly or in combination. Students' existing knowledge and beliefs influence what they see, hear, or smell. This means that not all students will observe phenomena in the same way. Students' level of observation skill can be measured through class discussion about their investigations. As students develop their skill, they will extend their existing ideas and understanding of what they observe and become more critical and discerning in what they observe. If student observations are limited to labeling and naming parts on a commercial drawing, their observation skills will remain static.

It is suggested that students start with a large sheet of blank paper to both draw and comment on their observations. This simple activity, followed by sharing and a class discussion, will usually lead students to make more observations to revise their initial perceptions. Classroom teachers recognize that information can come in pictures as well as in words, and more usually in the kind of text that combines images with words (Moline 1995). Teachers should consider several strategies to teach students how to read and write visual text. The development of this skill should begin in kindergarten with simple observations. Figure 8.1 is an example of a kindergarten student's perception of the relationship between the Sun, an object, and the resulting shadow created by the object. The teacher provided the students with large sheets of paper and asked the students to label their observations.

Figure 8.1
Kindergarten Student's Drawing of Shadows

In this example, the student demonstrates a correct understanding of the Sun-object-shadow relationship. It is interesting to note a common developmental mistake in learning to write is also illustrated here by the student reversing the "m" in sombra (which is shadow or shade in Spanish) to a "w." This drawing and writing assignment is also particularly effective with English learners as the students are using science vocabulary in a relational and contextual manner.

Another way teachers can assist students in writing their observations in their science notebooks is to allow students, especially young students, to glue or paste an example of their observation into their science notebook. Figure 8.2 is an example of a second-grade student's description of what he observed during a nature walk as an introduction to a unit on the study of plants. Note that the student has glued a leaf into his science notebook and then written a description of the leaf. There are limits in what should be pasted or glued into a science notebook. Pressed flowers are great for science notebooks. Large objects such as batteries and apparatus as well as living organisms should be avoided.

In this example, the student uses descriptive words to record observations of his evidence (the leaf). This is supported by Vygotsky's (1978) reference to drawing as graphic speech. These drawings can act as a guide to a student's understanding of science content. Students need time to develop the skill of self-expression and recording of observations. The teacher can guide students to record what they actually see and do, not what they think the teacher expects them to see or do. This allows the student to develop voice and construct meaning from their science instruction. Often students will draw their misconceptions. When done appropriately, drawings provide students with a means to shed their preconceptions and see what is actually there.

The development of the skill of recording observations through drawings progresses as students include more details and commentary related to the observation. Figure

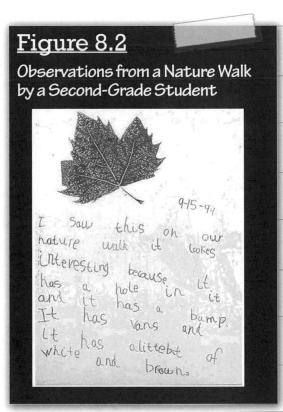

Figure 8.2
Observations from a Nature Walk by a Second-Grade Student

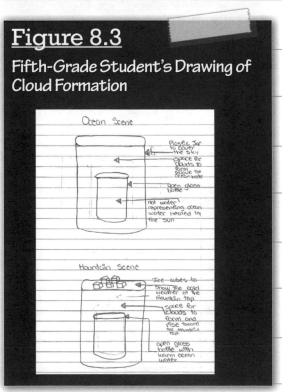

Figure 8.3
Fifth-Grade Student's Drawing of Cloud Formation

Observations, Data, Charts, Graphs, Drawings, and Illustrations

Figure 8.4

Fifth-Grade Student's Illustration of Evaporation

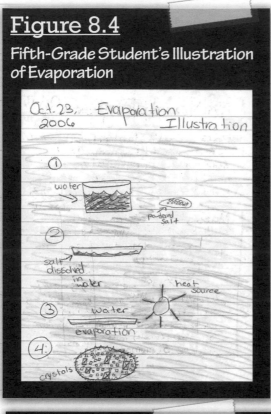

Figure 8.5

Fourth-Grade Student's Drawing of a Compass

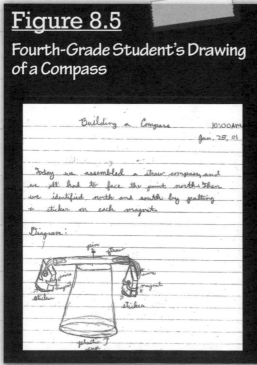

8.3 is a labeled drawing of how materials were assembled by a fifth-grade student conducting an investigation comparing cloud formation over the ocean and in the mountains.

The drawing and accompanying commentary demonstrate a developing student understanding of cloud formation, as Sun-heated moist warm air rises from the ocean and is cooled at higher elevations like mountaintops.

Figure 8.4 depicts the observed sequence of events that occurred in an investigation of making and evaporating a saltwater solution (physical change) by a fifth-grade student.

Note that the student has labeled each of the illustrations using the correct science terms as a scientist would.

Given the opportunity and time to draw or illustrate their observations, students develop the ability to observe more detail. Figure 8.5 is a fourth-grade student's labeled drawing and commentary of the construction of a compass in an investigation on magnetism and electricity. There is significant detail and good use of labeling in this drawing.

Figure 8.6 is a labeled illustration of an escapement clock drawn by a fifth-grade student.

Again there is significant detail and a good use of labeling in this drawing.

As stated, when students are given the time and opportunity to observe, illustrate, and label the details in their observation, deeper written comments start to emerge. Figures 8.7 and 8.8 are both examples of sixth-grade student observations of plant growth while they were conducting fair tests with Brassica plants.

In Figure 8.7 the student not only uses the drawing to depict her observation of the Brassica Plant, but also includes measurements of the seed pods in centimeters, predictions regarding the number of seeds in each pod, and a rich commentary regarding her developing understanding of these plants.

Figure 8.8 is a student record of observations taken the 16th day of an investigation. Here the student has also recorded a commentary of his measurements and a prediction of which plant (cell three) will bloom first based on the size of its buds.

The value in observing and recording details is that it helps students make meaning from their investigations. There is also value in observing similarities and differences. This can help students identify patterns or discover other properties. Figures 8.9a and 8.9b are a second-grade student's drawing and comments associated with an observation of crickets.

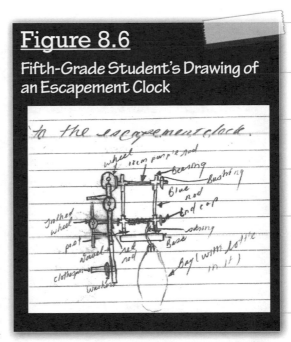

Figure 8.6
Fifth-Grade Student's Drawing of an Escapement Clock

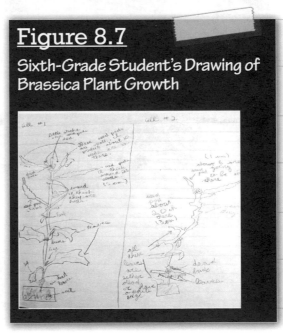

Figure 8.7
Sixth-Grade Student's Drawing of Brassica Plant Growth

The labeled drawings of the male and female crickets in Figure 8.9a clearly demonstrate an understanding of the similarities and differences in body structures on both insects. The student analysis of body structures in the observational chart in Figure 8.9b also displays the student understanding that crickets are insects.

Observations, Data, Charts, Graphs, Drawings, and Illustrations

Figure 8.8

Sixth Grade Student's Drawing of Brassica Plant Growth

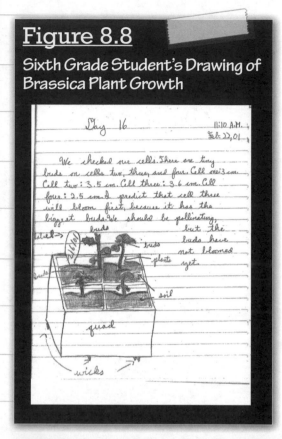

Observation can lead students to see patterns in the collected data. Figure 8.10 is an example of a fifth-grade student's collection of data related to tracking the path of the Sun during the school day. It is important to note that the student's prediction indicates a stage of thinking the student had before the investigation was conducted, while the analysis of the pattern of the data collected indicates that there was a definite change in student thinking as a result of this investigation. Note in this example that the student has the predicted outcome in conflict with the actual outcome. The teacher should plan to have students use the observation time to find patterns related to the evidence they collect. This can help the students form meaning through class discussion of the claims and associated evidence drawn from their science notebook entries.

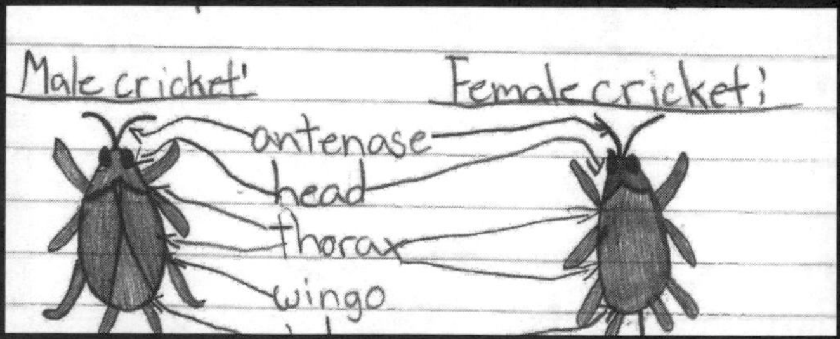

During the class discussion, the teacher asked the student why the whole graph in his entry (Figure 8.10) was backwards. The student responded that the observed direction that the Sun moves would not create the pattern predicted, but the pattern was just the opposite in terms of the shape of the curve of the pathway of the Sun. The quality of the observation is a significant factor in determining if a purposeful conclusion can be drawn. The value of the investigation for student conceptual understanding is strongly influenced by the quality of the observation.

Figure 8.9a

Second-Grade Student's Drawing of Crickets

Teacher questioning during the observation process can also play another role. As the teacher circulates between groups during the observation, the teacher should note whether certain critical details have been observed. This will help the teacher prompt students to describe what they have actually observed.

The quality of the observation can be enhanced by providing students with the opportunity to have sufficient time to observe. Classroom discussion plays an important role in this process. Teachers may ask a variety of questions to help refine the observation process and thus improve its quality. Appropriate types of questions teachers may ask include:

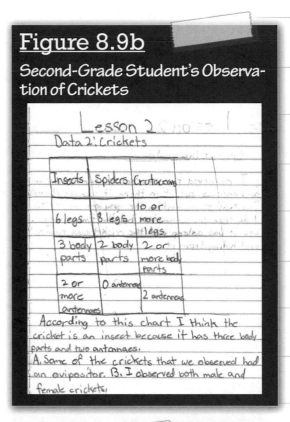

Figure 8.9b

Second-Grade Student's Observation of Crickets

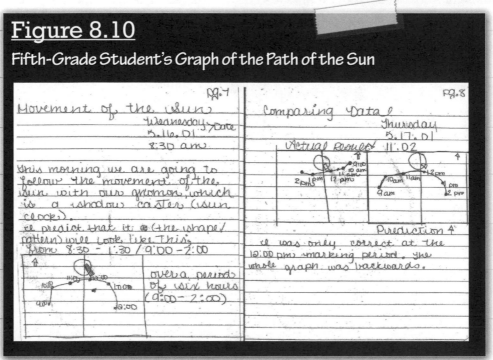

Figure 8.10

Fifth-Grade Student's Graph of the Path of the Sun

Observations, Data, Charts, Graphs, Drawings, and Illustrations

How are _____ the same as _____?

How are _____ different from _____?

What did you notice when you _____?

The development of the skill of observation can also include student ability to use equipment such as hand lenses and microscopes.

The key to improving observation skills in students comes from careful teacher planning. Teachers should consider organizing observation activities so students can talk in groups about what they observe, and whole class discussions in which groups or individual students share with the rest of the class what they have observed. Observation is a skill that students need to develop so that they can effectively learn from the objects and materials around them directly related to their investigation. In doing so, they have a greater opportunity to extend their thinking about a science concept, gathering data related to answering their focus question and drawing a conclusion from their investigation.

Tables, charts, and graphs are another important way for students to make meaning from their investigations. Prompts for the student development of data charts and tables were discussed in Chapter 7 as part of the planning process for their investigation. Students should be reminded that the data that is collected from their observations is their evidence for the investigation. Figure 8.11 is an example of a data chart completed by a fifth-grade student during an investigation of the properties of solids. This data chart will be used by the student later as evidence to support claims and draw conclusions.

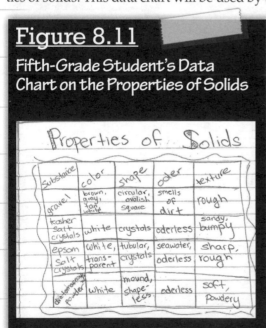

Figure 8.11
Fifth-Grade Student's Data Chart on the Properties of Solids

The data chart from another fifth-grade student depicted in Figure 8.12 indicates that solutions of kosher salt and water and Epsom salt and water have a mass equal to the sum of the mass from each of the components of the solution. This data will be used again later in the investigation to be compared to the mass of the salt remaining after evaporation occurs.

Figure 8.13 shows data from multiple trials of an investigation by a fifth-grade student. Chapter 7 discussed the value of multiple trials and averaging the data when taking measurements. This data chart is also supported by a series of labeled illustrations depicting the procedure followed for each trial.

In addition, once students have used these charts and tables to collect the data from their investigation, they may be guided to create graphs to represent their collected data. Teachers may use the following guiding questions to assist students in the development of data graphs:

From the types of graphs you know, which one is the most appropriate to show your data? Bar Graph? Line Graph? Pie Chart?

What are you going to name or title your graph?

What is the best way to show your data: scale, intervals, symbols?

For older students:

Where is your dependent and independent variable?

What are you going to name each axis?

Figures 8.14a and 8.14b are examples of how a fourth-grade student developed a graph showing the relationship between the force of two magnets when an increasing number of spacers is placed between them.

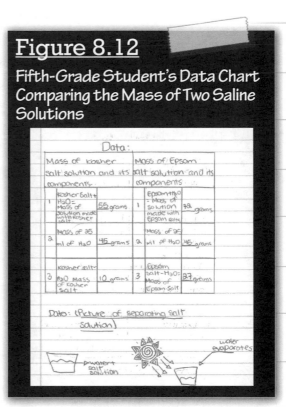

Figure 8.12

Fifth-Grade Student's Data Chart Comparing the Mass of Two Saline Solutions

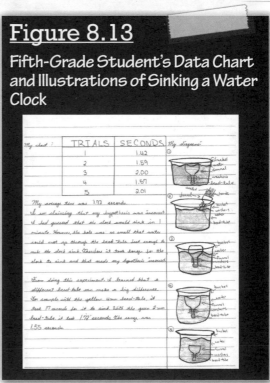

Figure 8.13

Fifth-Grade Student's Data Chart and Illustrations of Sinking a Water Clock

Observations, Data, Charts, Graphs, Drawings, and Illustrations

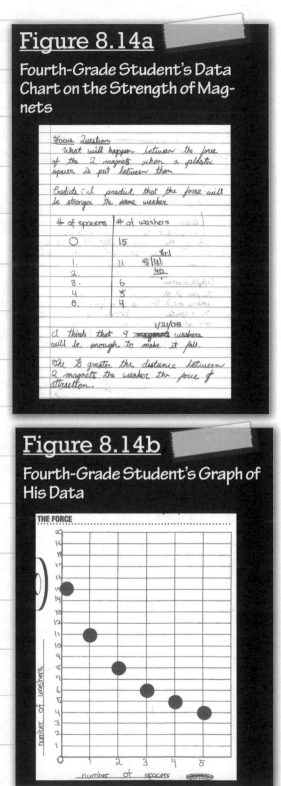

Figure 8.14a
Fourth-Grade Student's Data Chart on the Strength of Magnets

Figure 8.14b
Fourth-Grade Student's Graph of His Data

The student will later use the graph to support evidence and describe patterns and relationships discovered during the investigation.

In Figure 8.15, a fifth-grade student used two different types of graphs to represent the data from an investigation with water clocks.

Later, in a conference with the classroom teacher, the student discovered that the legend was reversed for both the double line and double bar graphs. The "unaltered experiment" was actually the experiment without changing the size of the bead in the funnel and the "altered experiment" changed the size of the bead in the funnel by 1 mm.

Another "teachable moment" was achieved when the classroom teacher discussed the bar graph shown in Figure 8.16 with the fifth-grade student who created it. The discussion focused on the use of fractions to depict parts of seconds. The class had recently been introduced to decimals during their mathematics lessons. The teacher asked the student to describe how intervals between seconds were depicted on the stopwatch used in the investigation. The student replied that the intervals were represented in tenths of seconds. After further consideration the student saw the connection between what he had learned in mathematics as an application to science.

Teachers can also introduce a cycle graph template to help students show how living things have different stages in their lives. A cycle graph template is depicted in Figure 8.17 (p. 58). Often young students will need this type of scaffold to assist them in their initial use of cycle graphs or life cycle charts because students are more used to a left-to-right progression of sequence in reading or a linear pattern as in a number line used in mathematics.

Figure 8.18 (p. 58) is an example of how a second-grade student used this template to record the life cycle of a butterfly, but still has not mastered the use of arrows to show direction of the life cycle.

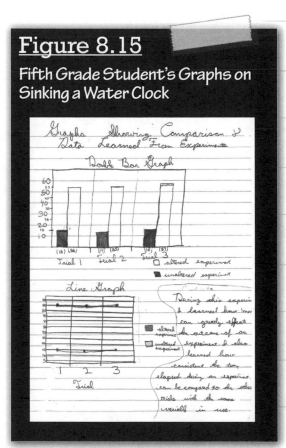

Figure 8.15

Fifth Grade Student's Graphs on Sinking a Water Clock

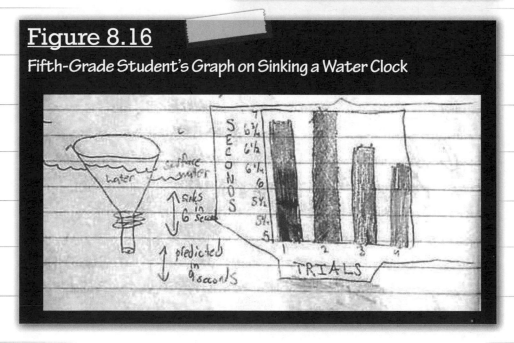

Figure 8.16

Fifth-Grade Student's Graph on Sinking a Water Clock

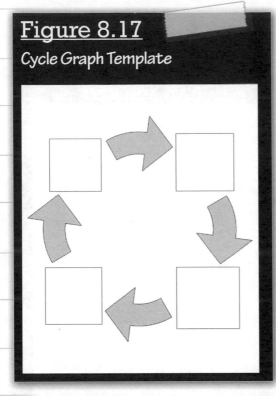

Figure 8.17
Cycle Graph Template

Graphic representations of data can be improved and misconceptions reduced through the use of teacher feedback. Teacher feedback will be discussed in greater detail in Chapter 15.

Observations, drawings, tables, charts, and graphs are essential elements that students must record in their science notebooks in order to make meaning from their investigations. These elements form the evidence of the investigation. Teachers should carefully scaffold the learning with prompts, questions, and templates necessary for students to adequately and accurately collect and record data. This evidence will later form the basis for making and supporting claims about the patterns and relationships that they have observed during the investigation.

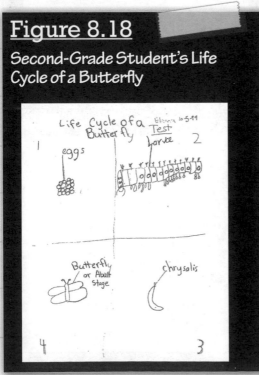

Figure 8.18
Second-Grade Student's Life Cycle of a Butterfly

Evidence-based explanations are a critical aspect of science. Teachers need to create classroom environments that support evidence-based scientific practices. Engaging students in explanation can change their image of science, enhance their understanding of the nature of science, and foster conceptual understanding. A deep understanding of science content is characterized by the ability to explain phenomena. Scientific explanations help frame the goal of inquiry as understanding natural phenomenon, and articulating and convincing others of that understanding.

Teachers face challenges in guiding students to develop evidence-based explanations. Students typically discount the data that

Claims and Evidence

they have collected if the data contradict their current thinking regarding their prediction or outcome of their investigation. Many student explanations include claims with little evidence or justification drawn from the data that they have collected or observed. Students have difficulty using appropriate evidence and connecting evidence to a claim. Revealing the underlying and implied framework of scientific explanation through supports can facilitate students' explanation construction.

Classroom teachers should consider an explanation framework that includes claims, evidence, and conclusions as a means of helping students develop the ability to use evidence-based explanations in communicating investigation results. In the explanation framework a claim is a deduction, pattern, or finding from the investigation. Evidence is the data itself, both observed and measured, in the form of data, or an analysis of labeled drawings and diagrams that were collected during the investigation. The conclusion is the justification that links the claim and evidence together.

The explanation framework makes the task explicit to students by dividing the task into manageable components. The first component is the introduction of a template for students to use in linking claims to evidence. This template can be written on the chalkboard by the teacher, copied in student science notebooks as a chart, or duplicated for student use and then stapled or pasted into the student science notebook. The template is a t-chart as depicted below:

With this template, students should be reminded that each claim must be supported with evidence, either measured or observed during the investigation and recorded in the data collection device that was constructed during the planning phase or from an analysis of labeled drawings and diagrams created during the investigation.

Figure 9.1 is an example of a fifth-grade student's t-chart linking claims to evidence in an investigation of mixtures and solutions. The evidence was taken from the data-collection device used during the investigation. Note how the student used "because" as a linking word between his claim and his evidence.

Claims	Evidence
I claim that... *or* I know that...	I claim this because... *or* I know this because...

The sentence starters "I claim…" and "I know this because…" appear in another fifth-grade student's t-chart (Figure 9.2) in which she describes her understanding of chemical change and compounds.

Many classroom teachers like to have their students transform their claims and evidence statements from the t-chart format into complete sentences using the sentence starters "I claim…" and "because…." Figures 9.3 and 9.4 (p. 62) are examples of how two fourth-grade students used these sentence starters to link their claims to the evidence that they collected during their investigations with magnetism and electricity.

In both of these examples the teacher used the sentence starters to

Figure 9.1

Claims and Evidence T-Chart for Mixtures and Solutions

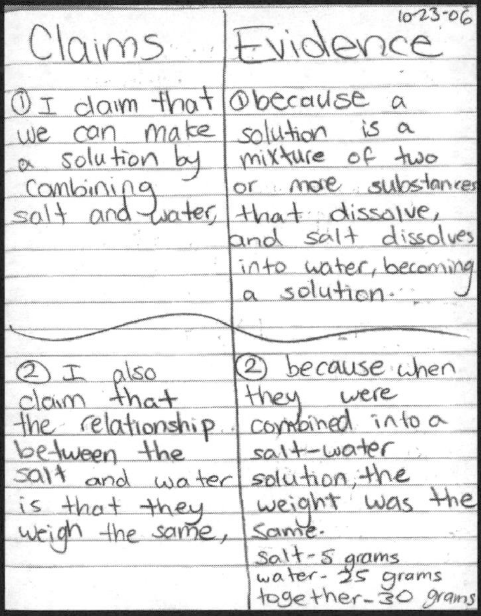

10-23-06

Claims	Evidence
① I claim that we can make a solution by combining salt and water,	① because a solution is a mixture of two or more substances that dissolve, and salt dissolves into water, becoming a solution.
② I also claim that the relationship between the salt and water is that they weigh the same,	② because when they were combined into a salt-water solution, the weight was the same. salt - 5 grams water - 25 grams together - 30 grams

Figure 9.2

Claims and Evidence T-Chart for Chemical Change

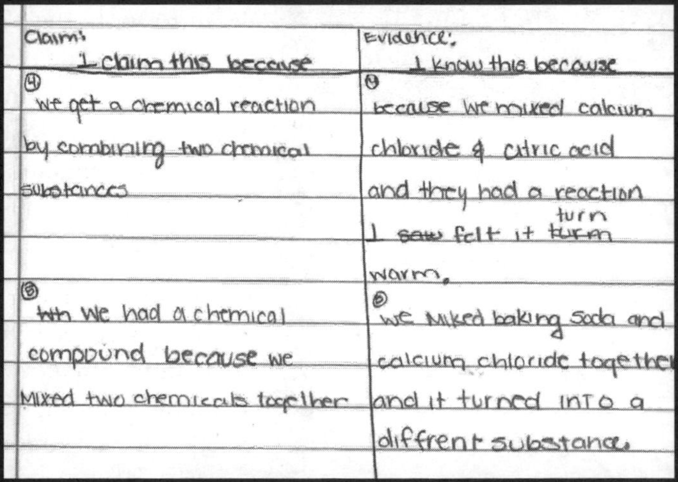

Claim: I claim this because	Evidence: I know this because
④ we get a chemical reaction by combining two chemical substances	④ because we mixed calcium chloride & citric acid and they had a reaction I ~~saw~~ felt it ~~turm~~ turn warm.
⑤ ~~wh~~ we had a chemical compound because we mixed two chemicals together	⑤ we mixed baking soda and calcium chloride together and it turned into a diffrent substance.

Figure 9.3

Claims and Evidence T-Chart and Sentences for Magnetism and Electricity

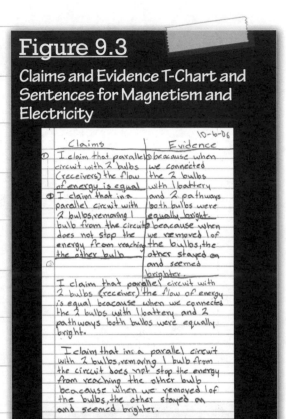

help students transition from filling in the t-chart to writing claims and evidence sentences. Students were prompted to use the left-hand side of the chart to complete the first part of the sentence "I claim that…." They were then prompted to use the right-hand side of their t-charts to complete the second part of the sentence "because…."

Given the opportunity and practice, students will transition from using the t-chart template and sentence prompts to constructing their own complete sentences comprised of their claims linked to their evidence. In Figure 9.5, a fourth-grade student has made this transition and is writing claims supported by evidence statements in his science notebook without the use of any of the supports.

Other students may begin to write statements about what they thought would happen before they learn to write their claims-linked-to-evidence statements. Figure 9.6 is an example of the discovery a fourth-grade student made regarding an investigation of what happened to the size of a balloon when exposed to hot and cold air.

One of the major goals for elementary science is for students to learn how to make evidence-based explanations regarding their investigations. Students can be assisted in this regard through the use of an explanation framework

Figure 9.4

Claims and Evidence T-Chart and Sentences for Magnetism and Electricity

that breaks the tasks into manageable components. T-chart templates, sentence starters, and transitional activities are important tools for teachers to use to assist their students in understanding, using, and reassembling these manageable components. These tools, along with class discussion and practice in their use, will greatly assist students in developing the skill necessary to write evidence-based explanations regarding their evidence or observations, and not simply what they did during the investigation. This shift is a prerequisite for students to develop a deeper understanding of the science content.

Figure 9.5
Claims and Evidence Sentences for Static Electricity

① I claim that static electricity is stationary but will attract an object with an opposite charge beacause when we rubbed the plastic bag or the balloon on the floor it became negatively charged and picked up the bits of paper that were positively charged.

② I claim that like charges (just as with like poles of a magnet) repel each other beacause when we rubbed 2 balloons on the carpet and then placed theme side by side, they moved apart

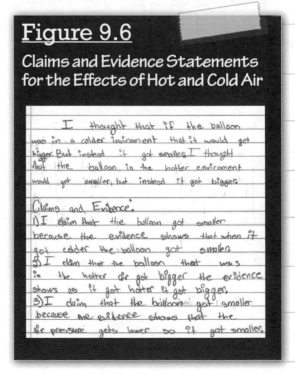

Figure 9.6
Claims and Evidence Statements for the Effects of Hot and Cold Air

I thought that if the balloon was in a colder inviroment that it would get bigger. But instead it got smaller I thought that the balloon in the hotter enviroment would get smaller, but instead it got bigger.

Claims and Evidence.
1) I claim that the balloon got smaller because the evidence shows that when it got colder the balloon got smaller
2) I claim that the balloon that was in the hotter air got bigger the evidence shows as it got hotter it got bigger.
3) I claim that the balloon got smaller because the evidence shows that the air pressure gets lower so it got smaller.

10 Drawing Conclusions

Drawing conclusions is the third component of an explanation framework of claims, evidence, and conclusions. This component is the justification that links the claim and evidence together. The student's justification explains why the data count as evidence to support the claim, using appropriate scientific ideas. When students use existing ideas to attempt to make sense of an investigation and their ideas change as a consequence, the conclusions they draw depend on the way in which their information was processed, how it was selected and recorded in the student science notebook, and how well claims were linked to the evidence.

Drawing Conclusions

Teachers need to assist students in interpreting and explaining their investigation results, while also helping them to reflect on their existing understandings. As students work in science, they are gathering data (evidence). Students can now refer to their data/observations/illustrations and claims and evidence entries in their student science notebooks to further develop their understanding about the science activity. This is one of the most difficult tasks for students because it pushes them to draw conclusions based on their own interpretations using the evidence collected during the investigation. Students must be guided to make sense of their data and examine what it means. Students need to use their claims and data to support their written and drawn conclusions.

Drawing conclusions requires students to put various pieces of information from their claims statements supported by the evidence they collected during the investigation. Jumping to conclusions is not the same as drawing conclusions. The evidence that was collected help form conclusions. This often involves students finding patterns in their results. Students should be asked to examine the evidence in their student science notebooks to determine what changed that led to other changes in the data collected. This is central to drawing conclusions. Students should be encouraged to examine the evidence they have collected and recorded in their student science notebooks and the claims that they have linked to their evidence to find a clear pattern. These patterns in claims linked to evidence will provide students with a systemic way of summarizing their findings to reach a conclusion.

In the primary grades, teachers can use the following sentence starters to help students with the formation of their conclusions:

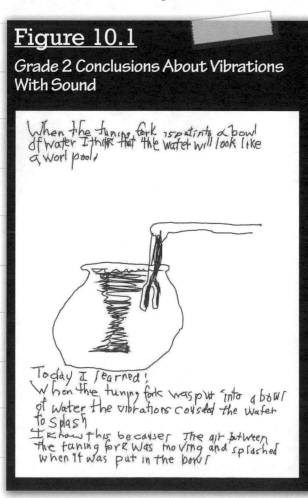

Figure 10.1
Grade 2 Conclusions About Vibrations With Sound

When the tuning fork is put into a bowl of water I think that the water will look like a worl pool.

Today I learned:
When the tuning fork was put into a bowl of water the vibrations coused the water to splash
I know this becauser The air between the tuning fork was moving and splashed when it was put in the bowl

Today I learned….

I know this
because….

Figure 10.1 is an example of a second-grade student using the sentence starters to draw a conclusion during an investigation of sound waves from a tuning fork.

Note that the student has also used a visual drawing with the use of lines to characterize the vibrations and used this to help form a conclusion.

A fifth-grade student describes her understanding of the six major bone groups and their functions in Figure 10.2. This understanding would be possibly strengthened with the use of a labeled drawing, as it will help the student to draw conclusions from her claims and evidence.

In Figure 10.3, a fourth-grade student displayed his understanding of the pattern of the number of washers a magnet can attract by increasing the strength of the magnet by adding more magnets to form a larger magnet cluster.

Classroom discussions are useful for students to hear the claims supported by evidence from other students in forming their own conclusions. Students must also be guided to under-

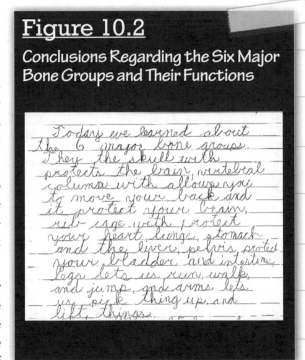

Figure 10.2
Conclusions Regarding the Six Major Bone Groups and Their Functions

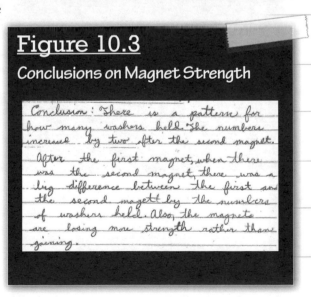

Figure 10.3
Conclusions on Magnet Strength

stand that their individual or group results may be different from others. This is because not all patterns are regular. Teachers need to guide students to understand that they cannot just ignore data that do not fit an exact pattern. Figure 10.4 (p. 68) is a second-grade student's conclusion drawn from an investigation

Drawing Conclusions

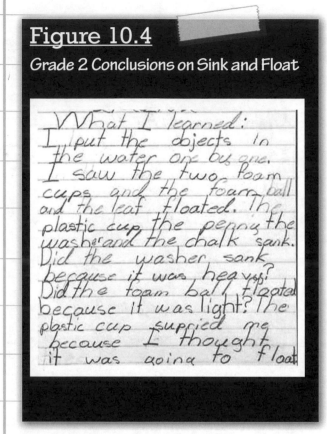

Figure 10.4
Grade 2 Conclusions on Sink and Float

> What I learned:
> I put the objects in the water one by one. I saw the two foam cups and the foam ball and the leaf floated. The plastic cup the penny, the washer and the chalk sank. Did the washer sank because it was heavy? Did the foam ball floated because it was light? The plastic cup supried me because I thought it was going to float

Figure 10.5
Grade 3 Conclusions About Rocks

> 12:45   October 2, 1998
>
> I learned that rocks can be hard and soft. Rocks also can be all different colors. Rocks can be shaped in any way. Some rocks have sharp eges. Some rocks can write. Rocks are bumpy. Rocks can sparkle. Rocks can have lots of layers. Rocks are heavy.

of the ability of objects to sink or float and how he was surprised by one of the objects.

This understanding could lead students to be guided to replicate their investigation, examine their plan, or realize that replication is important in looking for patterns in data. This will help reduce student misconceptions regarding the data that they have collected.

A conclusion can also be viewed as a summary statement of what was learned by students as a result of the investigation recorded in their science notebooks. This summary then becomes a permanent record that can be revisited by the student later in the unit of study. Figure 10.5 is an example of a summary statement recorded by a third-grade student regarding her current understanding of different types of rocks and minerals. Note that the student has not yet been exposed to sedimentary, metamorphic, and igneous rock types, but developmentally has identified certain characteristics in rocks that will later become useful when these rock types are introduced in later grades. This notebook entry is also an example of how the student science notebook is actually a work in progress of the student's current understanding of science content, one that can be later referred to, updated, and modified as student understanding becomes more refined.

Good conclusions can be written by students at the earliest grade levels. Figure 10.6 is a conclusion reached by another third-grade student regarding only one rock type, igneous, accompanied by two descriptive examples of igneous rocks. This conclusion is a good example of student understanding of igneous rocks. The descriptive examples of pumice and obsidian display the depth of current understanding.

Another third-grade student writes about his understanding of the relationship between rocks and minerals in Figure 10.7.

A second-grade student writes a conclusion in her science notebook in Figure 10.8. She states the conditions necessary that she discovered for a clay boat to hold the most cargo (paper clips).

A kindergarten student writes a conclusion about the ability of different types of balls to bounce, including an explanation, in Figure 10.9 (p. 70).

The process of inference takes interpreting data further than just looking at patterns in numbers, to suggesting relations that account for the existence of the patterns. Figure 10.10 (p. 70) is an example of a fourth-grade student's understanding of how an electric motor works based upon the evidence that she collected dur-

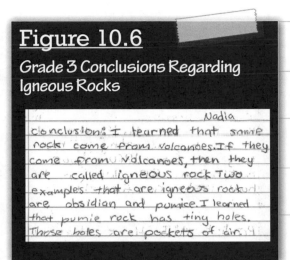

Figure 10.6
Grade 3 Conclusions Regarding Igneous Rocks

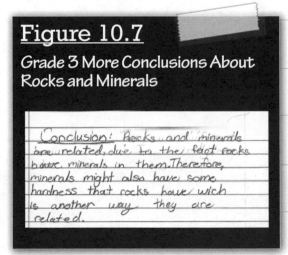

Figure 10.7
Grade 3 More Conclusions About Rocks and Minerals

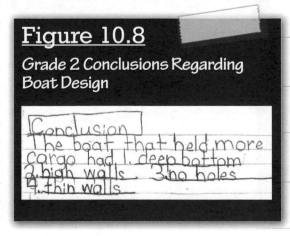

Figure 10.8
Grade 2 Conclusions Regarding Boat Design

Drawing Conclusions

Figure 10.9

A Kindergarten Student's Conclusion About Ball Bouncing

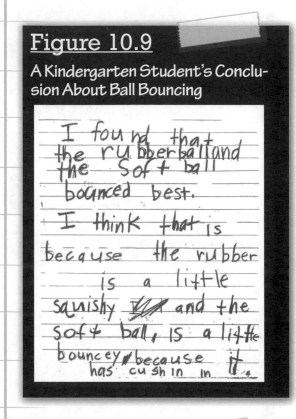

I found that the rubber ball and the soft ball bounced best.

I think that is because the rubber is a little squishy and the soft ball, is a little bouncey because it has cushin in it.

Figure 10.10

Fifth Grade Student's Conclusion About Electric Motors

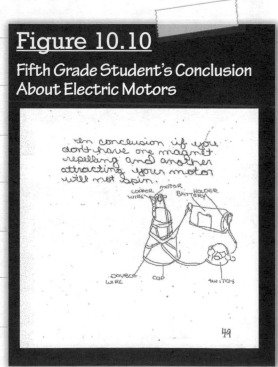

ing the investigation. The concept of how an electric motor works and the "big idea" that magnetism and electricity are part of a single force is evident in this conclusion.

A fourth-grade student concludes in Figure 10.11 that two bulbs can burn equally bright by only using one battery if one created a parallel circuit, which demonstrates a developing understanding of parallel circuits.

Teachers should also encourage students to revisit their predictions when writing a conclusion in their science notebooks. This exercise is intended to help students build new content knowledge by either revising or affirming their original prediction and to purge any existing misconceptions. Figure 10.12 is a conclusion reached by a fourth-grade student when she revisited and revised her prediction regarding the properties of matter.

In Figure 10.13, another fourth-grade student revisited his original prediction and affirmed it, regarding his understanding of evaporation of solutions. These examples reinforce the importance of students revisiting their original prediction to either affirm or revise as a means of developing a deeper understanding of science content.

A conclusion is the final "answer" to the focus question or the solution to the problem identified at the beginning of the investigation. Some teachers have characterized the process of investigative science in the following way: The focus question and prediction are the "what" of the investigation; the plan is the "how" of the investigation; and the claims, evidence, and conclusion of the investigation are the "so what." Drawing conclusions involves comparing initial ideas with new evidence and then deciding whether the ideas fit or need to be changed. It is the key to the investigation, where mental and practical activity comes together. This is how scientists approach investigative science and how classroom teachers should guide their students to do the same.

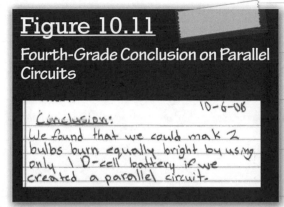

Figure 10.11

Fourth-Grade Conclusion on Parallel Circuits

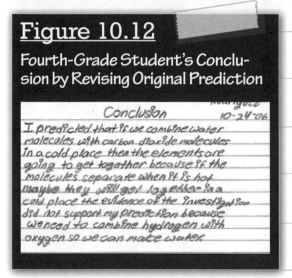

Figure 10.12

Fourth-Grade Student's Conclusion by Revising Original Prediction

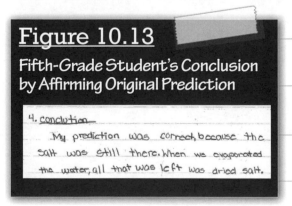

Figure 10.13

Fifth-Grade Student's Conclusion by Affirming Original Prediction

CHAPTER 11

Reflection: Next Steps, New Questions

Science investigations usually begin with students seeking an answer to a question or the solution to a problem. Similarly, after conducting a science investigation, students will have new questions. The outcome of the science investigation may stimulate students to think of new questions that they would like to investigate regarding the topic being studied. Teachers should encourage students to think of any new questions that they may have as a result of their conclusions or something regarding the investigation that still has been unanswered or not resolved and record them in their science notebooks. Just as when framing initial questions for the investigation, the questions should be investigable.

Reflection: Next Steps, New Questions

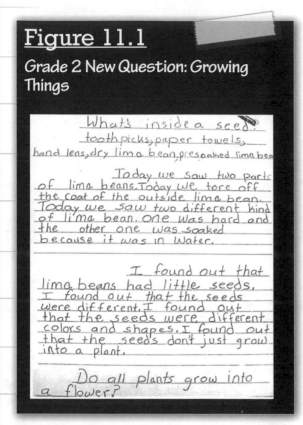

Figure 11.1
Grade 2 New Question: Growing Things

What's inside a seed?
toothpicks, paper towels, hand lens, dry lima bean, presoaked lima bean

Today we saw two parts of lima beans. Today we tore off the coat of the outside lima bean. Today we saw two different kind of lima bean. one was hard and the other one was soaked because it was in Water.

I found out that lima beans had little seeds. I found out that the seeds were different. I found out that the seeds were different colors and shapes. I found out that the seeds don't just grow into a plant.

Do all plants grow into a flower?

Figure 11.2
Grade 5 Reflection: Periodic Table

Reflection
1 How are elements classified or organized?
2 How can we combine the elements?
3 Are elements classified by electrons?

Teachers can help students frame questions just as they did in Chapter 5 by initially providing them with scaffolds such as What…?, Which…?, and How…? Questions that can be answered "yes" or "no" should be avoided. Figure 11.1 is an example of a second-grade student's question, "Do all plants grow into a flower?" formulated as a result of an investigation regarding what is inside a seed. While on the surface this is a "yes or no" type of question, the teacher used this question as an example of one that can be rewritten into an investigable question. After a classroom discussion of this question the student rewrote it to read, "Which plants grow flowers?" and conducted research on the internet and in the library to follow up the investigation they had just conducted.

Helping students turn "yes" or "no" questions into better questions that are investigable is an important role for classroom teachers.

A typical type of student reflection is listing several additional questions that have now become interesting to them as a result of the investigation. Figure 11.2 is a series of new questions raised by a fifth-grade student regarding elements as a result of an investigation related to the periodic table.

After discussion with the student, the teacher guided the student to select one of these questions to investigate further. The student chose the first question, "How are elements classified and organized?" and conducted an investigation that led to a deeper understanding of the periodic table. The quality of the reflection was based on the initial introduction to the periodic table from the investigation and the student's desire to learn more about the classification of elements. This self-selecting new investigation gave the student a personal interest in the topic and resulted in the student developing deeper understanding. Teachers should use these types of science notebook entries to assist students in conducting independent investigations or research related to the desired topic.

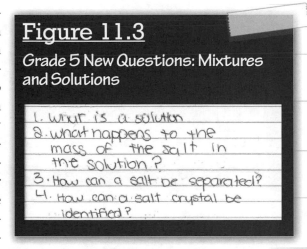

Figure 11.3

Grade 5 New Questions: Mixtures and Solutions

1. What is a solution
2. what happens to the mass of the salt in the solution?
3. How can a salt be separated?
4. How can a salt crystal be identified?

Another fifth-grade student listed a series of new questions (Figure 11.3) as a result of conducting an initial investigation related to making a saline solution.

After discussion with the student, the teacher guided the student to select one question to investigate. The student selected "How can salt be separated [from a saline solution]?" With the teacher's guidance, the student conducted an independent investigation on evaporation to determine if the salt could be separated from a saline solution. Again, the use of reflection and new questions provided the student with an opportunity to deepen her understanding of science content.

Sentence starters are an excellent way for teachers to prompt students to begin the reflection process. An example of a fourth-grade student's reflection using the sentence starter "I wonder what would happen if…?" is found in Figure 11.4. In his reflection question, the student is wondering what would happen if the variable of number of bulbs used in the investigation were changed from two to three.

After conducting a follow-up investigation, the student found that by increasing the number of bulbs from two to three in a parallel circuit still made three bulbs burn

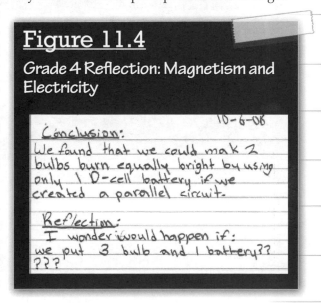

Figure 11.4

Grade 4 Reflection: Magnetism and Electricity

10-6-06
Conclusion:
We found that we could mak 2 bulbs burn equally bright by using only 1 D-cell battery if we created a parallel circuit.

Reflection:
I wonder would happen if:
we put 3 bulb and 1 battery??
???

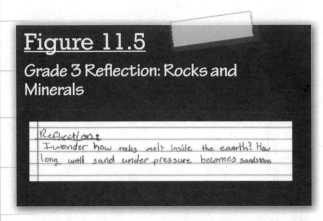

Figure 11.5

Grade 3 Reflection: Rocks and Minerals

> Reflection:
> I wonder how rocks melt inside the eaarth? How long until sand under pressure becomes sandstone

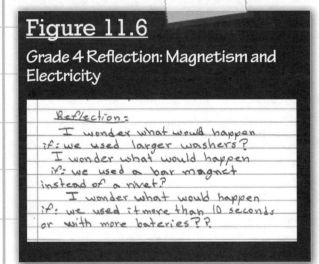

Figure 11.6

Grade 4 Reflection: Magnetism and Electricity

> Reflection:
> I wonder what would happen if: we used larger washers?
> I wonder what would happen if: we used a bar magnet instead of a rivet?
> I wonder what would happen if: we used it more than 10 seconds or with more bateries??

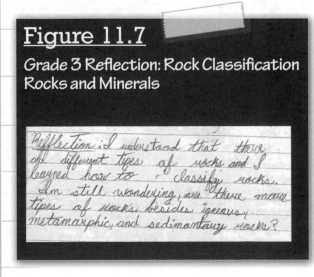

Figure 11.7

Grade 3 Reflection: Rock Classification Rocks and Minerals

> Reflection: I understood that there are different tipes of rocks and I learned how to classify rocks. I'm still wondering, are there more tipes of rocks besides igneous, metamorphic, and sedimantary rocks?

equally bright in a parallel circuit. This independent investigation greatly deepened the student's understanding of the nature of parallel circuits.

Using the beginning sentence starter, a third-grade student wonders in Figure 11.5 how rocks melt inside the earth. This question led the student to conduct additional research on the internet related to the Earth's core and rock formation.

The reflection questions can become proposals for new investigations that take the thought process further into the science concept being studied. A fourth-grade student wonders in Figure 11.6 what would happen if the variables they identified in an electromagnets investigation were changed. The student changed the variable of washer size and discovered that fewer large washers were picked up compared to the smaller washers, using the same numbers of winds of wire around the bolt in the electromagnet. Again, this independent investigation deepened the student's understanding of magnetism and electricity.

A third-grade student wonders if there are more than three types of rocks (Figure 11.7). This "wondering" question led the student to do additional library research on rock types. The student concluded that there were only three rock types.

In Figure 11.8, a fifth-grade student wonders if solutions become permanent. After conducting an independent investigation, the student concluded that some compounds in a solution can be separated and returned to their original form through evaporation and some cannot (physical change and chemical change). The student also concluded that if a solution were placed in a sealed airtight container, it may remain a solution.

Figure 11.9 is an example of a fourth-grade student's curiosity about circuits. The student is also highly motivated to seek an answer to his new question. Teachers should capitalize on this high level of student motivation and provide students with expanded opportunities to explore and deepen their understanding of science content.

A fifth-grade student is interested in replicating her investigation of removing substances from a solution through separation or filtration by changing the salt used in the investigation to sugar (Figure 11.10). This is a good example of student interest in repeating the initial investigation and changing one variable (salt to sugar), a curiosity to determine if they will attain the same results.

If students are asked to think of new questions, teachers should give students the opportunity to investigate these questions. This can usually

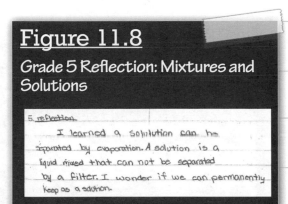

Figure 11.8

Grade 5 Reflection: Mixtures and Solutions

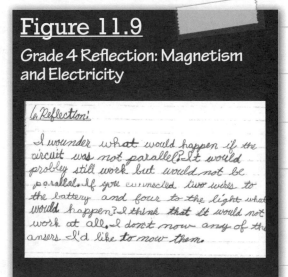

Figure 11.9

Grade 4 Reflection: Magnetism and Electricity

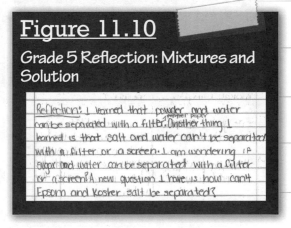

Figure 11.10

Grade 5 Reflection: Mixtures and Solution

Reflection: Next Steps, New Questions

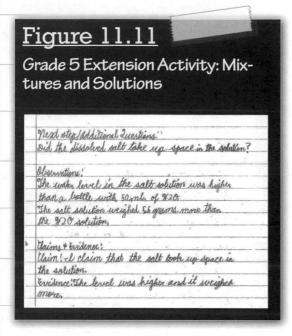

Figure 11.11

Grade 5 Extension Activity: Mixtures and Solutions

be addressed by setting up a center with the materials used in the initial investigation and allowing students to conduct a follow-up or extension to the investigation on their own. Students should be encouraged to write their findings in their science notebooks. Figure 11.11 is an example of a fifth-grade student's question and subsequent extension of the original investigation of whether salt dissolved in water increased the weight and volume of the water. The teacher discussed this "yes or no" type question with the student and the student subsequently changed the question to, "How did the dissolved salt take up space in the solution?" The student then independently constructed the follow-up investigation and listed his observations, claims, and evidence.

Classroom teachers also should find time to have students share these follow-up or extension investigations with the rest of the class. This new information will extend the knowledge base for all students in the class.

Finally, some teachers like to have their students write reflections about their investigation in their science notebooks by returning to their initial question and subsequent prediction and either affirm or revise that prediction, summarizing what they have learned, and explaining how their ideas have changed. This concept was discussed in Chapter 10 also as a means of helping students draw a conclusion from their investigation by revisiting and revising or affirming their initial prediction. The revisiting of the prediction is an important way to build new understanding and to guide students to reflect

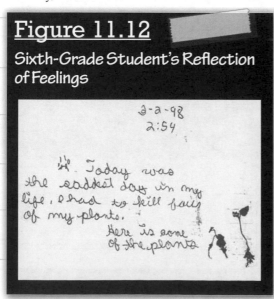

Figure 11.12

Sixth-Grade Student's Reflection of Feelings

on their work. This strategy of revisiting the prediction also allows for good self-assessment by the student and assessment opportunities for the teacher.

Students will often share their feelings as a part of the reflection process. A sixth-grade student shares her feelings after thinning some plants in an investigation of plant growth and development in Figure 11.12.

Written reflection is essential to promote student's explorations of their own thinking and learning processes, but is often omitted if science notebooks are used primarily as logs for procedures and observations of their learning activities. This final writing entry draws closure to the investigation and prepares the student to move on to the next investigation in the science unit. Reflection not only brings closure, but also allows for interpretation and critical review of the evidence, as is done by scientists.

CHAPTER 12

English Language Development and the Science-Literacy Connection

Public schools in the United States are educating a student population more diverse than ever before. With the national trend of standards, assessment, and accountability, school districts, schools, and classroom teachers face new challenges to provide these students with an opportunity to learn. Teachers face the challenge of developing English language fluency in students in the context of science content without diminishing or "watering down" the content. Classroom teachers well informed of "best practices" in English Language Development (ELD) can provide English Language Learners with the opportunity to learn and the ability to make meaning from their science classroom experiences through writing in science and through the effective use of science notebooks.

English Language Development and the Science-Literacy Connection

These ELD and writing strategies are designed to meet the needs of English Language Learners in the context of Standards-based science content attainment. This context will address the different levels of language acquisition directly related to the language needs of these students in order for teachers to better understand and meet the needs of their diverse student population.

Educating English Language Learners can be overwhelming, yet manageable with the help of specific strategies. Many of these strategies are especially advantageous to science learning. English Language Learners may be lacking specific linguistic skills, but at the same time they bring with them their own prior knowledge and experiences that can enhance the learning process. Strategies such as providing step-by-step instructions, posting terms/vocabulary where they are visible, rephrasing statements while checking for clarity, and actively involving students with peers or group work are just some that may be employed.

ELD applications integrated into science instruction provide excellent opportunities for students to make connections to science content and process skills. The primary application that provides a foundation for all areas is vocabulary building. As long as the vocabulary is coherent and introduced in context to the students, they will conceptualize word meanings and therefore make concrete connections. The context in which vocabulary is used cannot be emphasized too much here. There are several concrete relational and contextual strategies teachers can utilize to develop vocabulary.

One way vocabulary building is developed is through an interactive process of discussing science materials with students prior to a lesson or unit in which the students will be using these items. As the vocabulary is discussed, a record is kept. This record may be in a student's individual science notebook, but preferably on a working "word wall" developed by the teacher while the vocabulary is being introduced to the students.

A working word wall is composed of vocabulary that is directly related to the items and concepts being taught in the unit. As the teacher feels the need to introduce or review vocabulary with students, they write the word on chart paper, sentence strips, etc., and place it in clear view of all students.

Developing working word walls and charts in the classroom are extremely important for all students but even more so for English Language Learners. A working word wall assists these students in developing an understanding of—and fluency in—using key unit vocabulary. The visibility of the working word wall enables English Language Learners to use it as a reference when collaborating within a group and during class discussions. The working word wall empowers them when writing. The working word wall acts as a resource area accessible to all students.

Figure 12.1 is an example of a notebook entry from a second-grade student that was recorded from a working word wall prior to conducting an investigation on "sink and float." The student used this vocabulary in future science notebook entries when conducting investigations in this unit of study. There are some limitations in the use of this method alone, as there are no anchor points or definitions for future reference.

A fifth-grade student recorded vocabulary (Figure 12.2) in context prior to the start of a unit of study on the properties of matter. The student also listed some simple definitions for the vocabulary for future reference. Simple definitions, drawings, or other anchor points are important contextual reference points for English Language Learners to draw from in the use of scientific vocabulary.

Another strategy for contextual vocabulary development that classroom teachers can utilize is the kit inventory. It is more robust than just the working word wall alone. The objective of a kit inventory is to convert the materials found in a science kit that will be used during a unit of study into an active experience where students question and discuss the scientific names, use(s), and property description of these items. The kit inventory provides an excellent opportunity for students to build vocabulary in a coherent and contextual way.

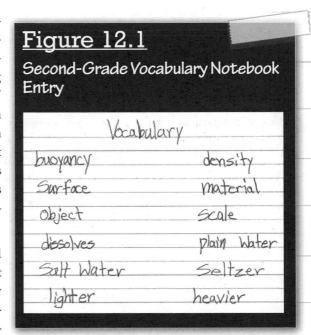

Figure 12.1

Second-Grade Vocabulary Notebook Entry

Vocabulary

buoyancy	density
Surface	material
Object	Scale
dissolves	plain water
Salt Water	Seltzer
lighter	heavier

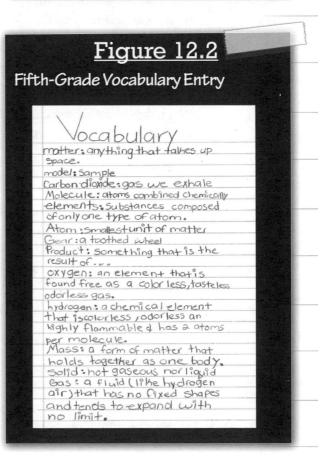

Figure 12.2

Fifth-Grade Vocabulary Entry

Vocabulary

matter: anything that takes up space.
model: sample
Carbon dioxide: gas we exhale
Molecule: atoms combined chemically
elements: substances composed of only one type of atom.
Atom: smallest unit of matter
Gear: a toothed wheel
Product: something that is the result of...
oxygen: an element that is found free as a colorless, tasteless odorless gas.
hydrogen: a chemical element that is colorless, odorless an highly flammable & has 2 atoms per molecule.
Mass: a form of matter that holds together as one body.
Solid: not gaseous nor liquid
Gas: a fluid (like hydrogen air) that has no fixed shapes and tends to expand with no limit.

English Language Development and the Science-Literacy Connection

Building the conceptual knowledge of what the items are, of their use or function, of where they came from, and how they are related to science is important in order for students to make meaning from their experiences.

The students can then organize the vocabulary into word clusters. The basic premise behind this process is to develop relational and contextual identification of the vocabulary as it will be used within the unit of study. The function behind a kit inventory activity is to introduce the unit to the students and to provide integration between science and ELD. Through a variety of methods a teacher can lay a conceptual foundation for language acquisition for students through their own descriptions and prior knowledge as to why these items are in their science kit. During this activity, the teacher constructs a working word wall with the name of the items, their synonyms, illustrations, and descriptions with the students.

There are different methods teachers can use to inventory a science kit. One strategy is to ask students to make predictions as to how an item will be used within the unit by removing one item at a time from the kit and asking the students to identify the item, discuss the item in terms of what it reminds them of, and then make a prediction as to the use of the item in the unit of study. If the kit inventory activity was related to a unit on rocks and minerals, a discussion could be as follows:

Item	Teacher Questions	Student Responses
Goggles	What are these? What are they made of? Where have you seen them before? Why do people have them at the swimming pool? Why do you think they are in our science kit?	Goggles. Plastic. At the swimming pool. To cover their eyes. To cover our eyes.
Nail	What is this called? When do you normally see these? What do you do with a nail? Look at this nail. The ends are different. What can you tell me about it? Do you have any predictions about what we might study in this unit?	A nail. When we are building. Pound it; put it in wood. One end is flat, one end is sharp. Maybe building.
Paper clip	What is this item called? Why are paper clips in our kit? What do you think we are going to be studying?	Paper clip. To hold paper together. Building.

The teacher would then place the item in a clear plastic bag, pin it to a bulletin board, and then pin a name label under the item. This expands the function of the working word wall and provides a visual example next to the written name of the object. This can serve as a valuable anchor point for vocabulary use by the student for the entire unit.

Figure 12.3 is an excerpt of a fifth-grade student's science notebook entry as a result of a kit inventory prior to an investigation of mixtures and solutions. Note that she not only listed the vocabulary naming the item, but also illustrated the item and then listed what she thought the item would be used for in the unit. The student can refer to this list throughout the investigation.

Another fifth-grade student simply listed the vocabulary introduced from an examination of objects during a kit inventory and made a prediction in Figure 12.4.

In comparing the two samples of student work resulting from a kit inventory, the process used by the classroom teacher requiring the student to record the item, illustrate the item, and predict what its use in the unit will be provided the students with useful anchor points for future reference and a much richer experience in the contextual use of the vocabulary.

The sentence stem introduced in Chapter 4 is an important tool to use to introduce English language learners to writing about their science experiences and to make meaning about what they have learned. Examples of these sentence stems include the following:

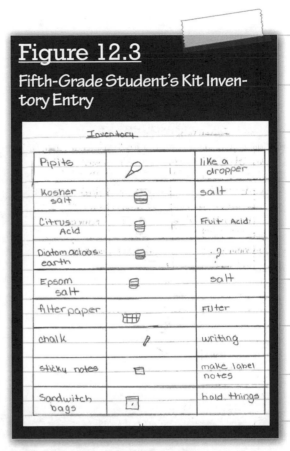

Figure 12.3
Fifth-Grade Student's Kit Inventory Entry

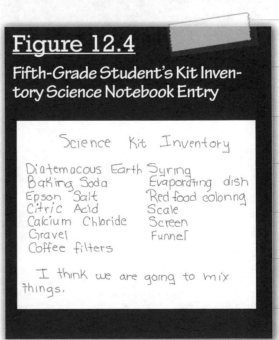

Figure 12.4
Fifth-Grade Student's Kit Inventory Science Notebook Entry

English Language Development and the Science-Literacy Connection

I wondered....

Today I learned....

I noticed....

My new question is....

Sentence stems provide an excellent starting point for students to begin writing about their science experiences, modeling correct grammar and sentence structure. Students can select key vocabulary from the working word wall to help complete these sentence stems. Students should record these in their science notebooks in order to maintain a permanent record of their progress and as a means to make meaning from their science experiences.

For example, after the development of word walls or charts, a teacher may say, "Today, after this investigation, I would like for you to write a reflection on the results of your investigation. Use the sentence stem 'Today I learned...' to start your writing. You will need to take four words from the working word wall and include them in your writing for today."

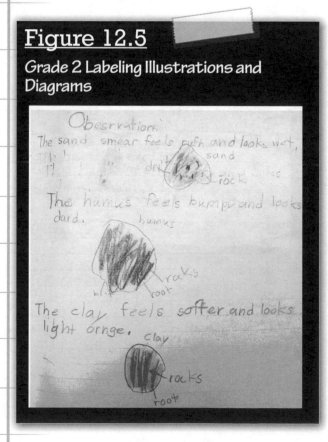

Figure 12.5

Grade 2 Labeling Illustrations and Diagrams

Students need to be exposed to a variety of charts to select from when they are required to document or interpret their data. The teacher should model how to set up these charts and have a class discussion on how to read the information from the charts. The end result should be that the students have a library of different charts they can choose to use, depending upon the nature of the activity. The students will then become independent in examining their evidence and deciding how they are going to display it in their science notebooks. Students will prove to be successful if the vocabulary is set in a scaffolding method as opposed to just copying the word and definition from the teacher.

Labeling diagrams and illustrations also increases language acquisition and fluency. Student science notebook entries should contain drawings and illustrations of their activity just as real scientists do in their own science notebooks. Teachers should encourage students to label every illustration using the scientific vocabulary introduced in earlier lessons. This reinforces the use of language in context and builds relational values. Students should be encouraged to use vocabulary for their labels from the working word wall or word charts in the classroom.

A second-grade student's labeled illustration of soils in Figure 12.5 is a good example of the application of this principle. Note that the student has used arrows to connect the labels to the illustration of the soils.

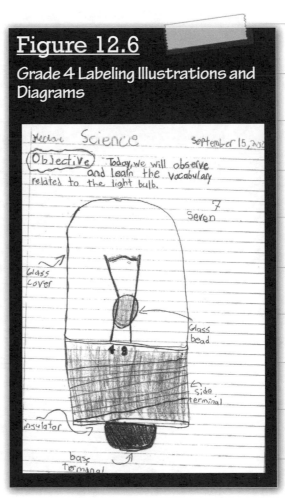

Figure 12.6

Grade 4 Labeling Illustrations and Diagrams

Another good example of student labeling is the fourth-grade student's labeled illustration of a light bulb in Figure 12.6.

In this example the student has used arrows to connect the vocabulary label to each part of the light bulb, has listed an objective, and has dated the notebook entry. Again, this can be used as a contextual reference point for later use in the unit of study.

In order for English Language Learners to effectively use scientific vocabulary in English in recording their investigations, it is important for teachers to use a variety of vocabulary-building activities within the context of experiential learning. It is equally important for English Language Learners to employ the scientific vocabulary in recording their investigations in their science notebooks in order to build understanding of the vocabulary in English and fluency in its use in their speaking and writing.

Additional Strategies for Increasing the Use of Academic Content Language in the Writing of English Language Learners

There are additional strategies classroom teachers need to consider with English Language Learners to help them develop scientific content vocabulary. Several of these strategies are not unique to science, but are drawn from language arts and are also excellent English Language Development practices. Strategies such as classification, sorting and classifying, Venn Diagrams, word charts, and cloze techniques are effective strategies for English Language Learners to use. The increase in the use of the scientific language in their writing and classroom discussion will increase their conceptual understanding.

Additional Strategies for Increasing the Use of Academic Content Language in the Writing of English Language Learners

Asking the students to classify the items in their science kit is an extension of the kit inventory activity described in Chapter 12. Taking all the items out of the kit and placing them in different groups that reflect the properties of the items is another strategy used by teachers to build relational concepts. The teacher may tap into the student's prior knowledge during the science kit inventory by asking questions such as, "Where have we seen this before? What have you seen it used for?" The discussion that develops from accessing student prior knowledge will allow the teacher to assess student understanding of vocabulary that will be used in the unit of study. Having students describe the items changes the focus to the properties of the items. The classification extension of the kit inventory activity provides opportunities for repetition of vocabulary and contextual understanding. For example, if the kit inventory activity was drawn from a unit on magnetism and electricity, the classification portion could have the following focus:

Conductors	Nonconductors
bolt	craft stick
wire	plastic bag
nail	plastic disk
paper clip	eraser
fastener	
screw	
penny	

Once the students feel comfortable with the definition/description/property of the items introduced during the kit inventory, a sorting and classifying activity may take place. Students sort the same items that were introduced for the working word wall during the kit inventory. Students will apply their prior knowledge of the properties of the items and discuss these properties within their groups, and in a class discussion, explaining why the items have been sorted in a certain way. The teacher's goal is for the reinforcement of the properties through the use of these items. There is no right or wrong group category as long as the students can explain their reasoning and provide a justification for placing items in a certain group. An example is listed below to illustrate this strategy:

Group A   Man-made items

Group B   Natural items

or

Group A   Plastic

Group B   Metal

Teachers can follow up a sorting and classifying activity by asking students to explain how they have grouped the items. A second-grade student uses a chart to show how the items in a "sink and float" activity were sorted and classified in Figure 13.1.

Teachers can ask students to sort and classify or compare the characteristics of things by listing similarities and differences. Figure 13.2 is an example of a second-grade student listing the similarities and differences between humans and butterflies.

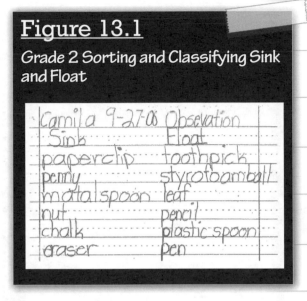

Figure 13.1

Grade 2 Sorting and Classifying Sink and Float

These strategies provide additional contextual and relational experiences for English Language Learners to acquire language and build fluency through repetition. Foundation building for these students at the beginning of the unit will encourage comfort with the vocabulary and confidence in its use throughout the entire science unit.

Another way of having students make comparisons or find either categories or groups in which they find similarities and differences is through the use of Venn diagrams. A Venn diagram is a pictorial representation of circles positioned to represent how groups of objects are the same (interlocking or overlapping of the circles) and how they are different (the portion of the circles not interlocking or overlapping). Pictorial representations of the similarities and differences in categories or groups of objects provide concrete examples for English Language Learners.

Venn diagrams can be developed using the items from the kit or

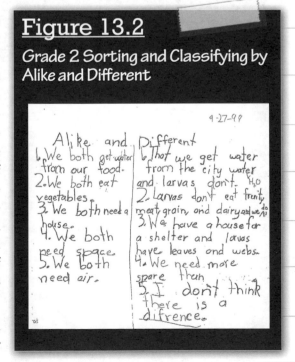

Figure 13.2

Grade 2 Sorting and Classifying by Alike and Different

Figure 13.3

Grade 3 Venn Diagram Comparing Rocks and Minerals

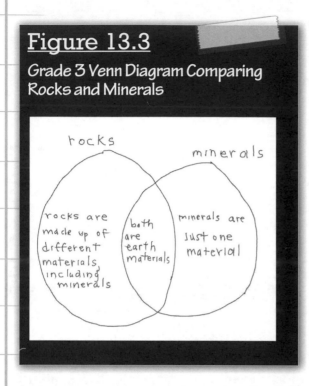

rocks   minerals

rocks are made up of different materials, including minerals

both are earth materials

minerals are just one material

Figure 13.4

Grade 5 Venn Diagram States of Matter

Oct. 6' 06   States of Matter

Venn Diagram

water
- transparent
- H2O -oderless
- liquid -def. vol.
- shapeless

Carbon Dioxide
- gas
- CO2
- invisible

- C6H2O6
- solid
- crystals
- dissolves

sugar

the names of the items printed on index cards. Hula hoops or large rings of yarn can be used to form the interlocking rings of the Venn diagram. Figure 13.3 is a third-grade student's Venn diagram depicting his understanding of the similarities and differences between rocks and minerals.

Figure 13.4 illustrates a fifth grade student's Venn diagram showing similarities and differences in describing states of matter.

Figure 13.5 is a Venn diagram a group of students created to show similarities and differences between series and parallel circuits.

Venn diagrams are a concrete means for students to develop and visualize their understanding of the similarities and differences between objects, use scientific vocabulary in context, and to build language fluency.

Word charts are different from working word walls. Word charts are clusters of words separated into categories. The categories that are commonly used for clusters include:

Figure 13.5
Grade 4 Venn Diagram Comparing Electric Circuits

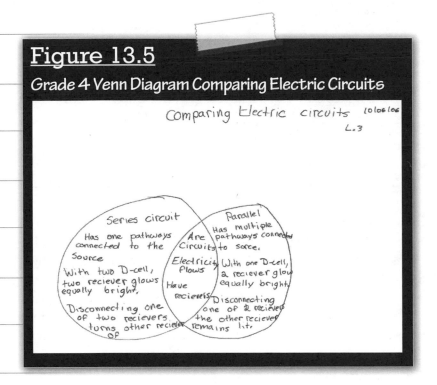

Comparing Electric circuits 10|06|06
                                    L.3

Series circuit
Has one pathways connected to the Source
With two D-cell, two reciever glows equally bright,
Disconnecting one of two recievers turns other recieler of

Are Circuits
Electricity flows
Have recieleis

Parallel
Has multiple pathways connected to sorce.
With one D-cell, a reciever glow equally bright,
Disconnecting one of 2 reciever the other reciever remains lit,

Science Process Vocabulary: mainly process skills

Content Vocabulary: dealing with the unit at hand

Additional Vocabulary: words that connect (*and, into, through*) when discussing the groups, or descriptive words

As teachers proceed through activities such as the science kit inventory or during any of the investigations or subsequent discussions, any new words or any words important for the students are placed in any one of these three categories. The building of vocabulary continues throughout the unit and throughout the year.

Science Process Vocabulary is important to develop and includes the prediction, what data looks like, and what it means to give evidence and write a reflection. Content Vocabulary refers to those words that are directly connected to the science unit of study (for example, rocks, minerals, sedimentary, igneous, and metamorphic). Additional Vocabulary includes words that connect, such as *on, in, around, inside, outside,* and so forth. English Language Learners often have a difficult time in using words that connect when writing sentences. After teachers have developed these charts, they are able to have students use words from each of these categories to begin writing sentences. This chart serves as a reference point for students to make connections between these three different categories and builds

Additional Strategies for Increasing the Use of Academic Content Language in the Writing of English Language Learners

fluency. A word chart from the beginning of a unit on magnetism and electricity could be constructed as follows:

Properties of the Objects	
Metal	screw, nail, compass, paper clip, fastener, wire
Flexible	wire, straw, fastener, paper clip, pipe cleaner
Nonmetal	straw, craft stick, pipe cleaner, plastic bag, Tinker Toy
Connecting Words	in, on, into, between, above, below

Cloze paragraphs are a strategy to use language in context. It is an instructional strategy in which key scientific vocabulary is deleted from a passage. The passage is then presented to students, who insert scientific vocabulary as they read to complete the passage. Cloze sentences and paragraphs can be developed by teachers using vocabulary from the working word wall or word charts. The teacher may require as part of the rubric for a writing assignment that a minimum of four words from the working word wall be used correctly to complete the sentences in the passage. An example of a cloze paragraph for a unit on rocks and minerals is shown below:

penny   gypsum   quartz   tools   mineral   nail

We found that some minerals could be scratched and some could

not. The _____ was the hardest mineral because the _____ and the

_____ could not scratch it. _____ was the softest _____ because

all of our _____ could scratch it.

English Language Learners represent the fastest growing segment of the school population in the United States. There is not an entire set of best practices that are good for just English Language Learners, but in fact, many of the linguistically related approaches identified in this chapter can be used with all students in the class. English Language Learners can achieve success across the curriculum with the integration of language acquisition strategies that accommodate their needs. The primary goal for teachers working with English Language Learners is to consistently provide a contextual base for the introduction of vocabulary and sufficient repetition and practice through the use of a series of strategies like sorting, classifying, Venn diagrams, and cloze practice to build fluency.

The language of science and English are complementary and the integration of English Language Development in science is a natural way for English Language Learners to fully participate in a high-quality program of instruction in science and acquire proficiency in English through writing their science notebooks.

14 Assessing Student Progress

Teachers are in the best position to use assessment to improve classroom practice, plan instruction, develop competency in students and to reflect on their own teaching practices (NRC 1996). However, assessment practices in science in the elementary classroom have most often been relegated to end-of-unit tests provided by commercial textbooks. These are usually in the form of multiple-choice questions with answers that can be easily found, and sometimes even highlighted, in the unit itself. They are most often factual questions and rarely ones that require students to go beyond recall or engage in any type of critical thinking.

Assessing Student Progress

These types of assessments do not provide a good representation of the student's thinking about the concept studied or about how one student's thinking differs from that of his or her peers. These assessments also do not necessarily give teachers an indication that students understand science for the long term, as most questions relate directly back to what was just reviewed rather than what was experienced. Often these assessments are more a "test" of the student's ability to speak and read English rather than a measure of the student's conceptual or procedural understanding.

Traditional assessments often do not provide teachers with an opportunity to check for misconceptions that students may have, because the selection of one answer on a multiple-choice test does not offer insights as to why the student selected it.

The goals for school science projected in the National Science Education Standards represent a significant shift from traditional practice (NRC 1996). Teachers need to determine how well students are meeting these new goals. Student science notebooks can be used to both gauge student progress and to inform teaching and learning. This requires the classroom teacher to help students operate within three guiding questions suggested by the NRC (2001):

- *Where are you trying to go?* (Identify and communicate the learning and performance goals or standards)

- *Where are you now?* (Assess or self-assess current student levels of understanding)

- *How can you get there?* (Help the student with strategies and skills to reach the goal)

In an era of standards, assessment, and accountability, assessments linked to standards in the first guiding question reflect the complexity of science as a discipline of interconnected ideas as well as a way of thinking about the world. Assessment in the second guiding question is linked to teacher action in the third guiding question, resulting in formative assessment. Student science notebooks become an evolving record of the implementation or application of these guiding principles.

Student science notebooks then play an important role in the triad of what should be taught (standards), what is actually taught (classroom instruction) and what content students learn. In this context, the student science notebook is the means by which students communicate their understanding. The student science notebook is the best record of the depth of student content understanding and the quality of the communication of that understanding. Equally important, student science notebooks are effective assessment tools in specifically assessing student ability to formulate scientific explanations from evidence. These factors make student science notebooks an effective formative assessment tool for teachers in assessing student science conceptual understanding and complex reasoning. Formative assessments provide information to students and teachers that is used to improve teaching and learning. Recognizing that the acquisition of conceptual understanding and complex reasoning is developmental, student science notebooks can also be viewed as an effective assessment tool.

Entries in student science notebooks identify the gaps between where individual students are in their learning and where they need to be. Was the content standard actually understood by students in its relationship to a big idea in science? What was the quality of student communication and conceptual understanding? Similarly, classwide results inform teachers about the gaps and strengths in the lesson design.

Gaps between what was expected and what was accomplished are evidenced by comparing the criteria for each of the components in a student science notebook entry for the lesson to student entries or comparing the procedural and content understanding for the entire unit. Compliance with instructional expectations is balanced with allowance and recognition for science notebooks that are individually creative.

Teachers can begin the process of using student science notebooks as a formative assessment tool by asking themselves the following guiding questions:

> **What should all students learn in this unit? (content skills and/or process skills)**
>
> **How do the student science notebooks reflect student learning?**
>
> **What evidence should support their understandings? (criteria)**
>
> **What are the implications for further instruction?**

In answering these questions, teachers can use an assessment rubric similar to the one depicted in Figure 14.1 (p. 100) as a means of getting started.

This assessment rubric responds to the four principles for teachers to consider: (1) What should all students be expected to learn in this unit? is addressed in the "Big Idea"; (2) How do the science notebooks reflect student learning? is addressed in "What Have You Learned?" as well as "Next Steps/New Questions"; (3) What evidence should support their understandings? is addressed through the criteria identified for each of the headings; and (4) What are the implications for further instruction? is considered after each of the other three guiding questions or principles are addressed. Thus, the student science notebook becomes a central element for teachers to use in formative assessment to determine where the students are attempting to go, where they are now, and how you can help them get there.

Figure 14.1

Science Notebook Assessment Rubric

Elements and Criteria	NA	Not present	Lacking	Meets	Exceeds
Big Idea					
Question Purpose					
Student generated; in own words/ Relates to purpose/'Big Idea' Clear and concise Investigable	COMMENTS:				
Prediction					
Connects to prior experience Is clear and reasonable Relates to question Gives an explanation/reason	COMMENTS:				
Planning					
Relates to investigable question Has clear sequence/direction Identifies variables/control Includes data organizer States materials needed	COMMENTS:				
Data/Observations					
Relates to question and plan Includes student generated drawings, charts, graphs, narrative Organized Accurate	COMMENTS:				
What Have You Learned?					
Student generated: in own words Clear statement of what was learned Based on question/planning/evidence Reflective Shows rigor in thinking	COMMENTS:				
Next Steps/New Questions					
Student generated Extension/new application of original question Researchable or investigable WOW factor Can be recorded throughout	COMMENTS:				

Figure 14.2
Standards-Based Assessment Rubric

Measuring Time – Lessons 7-9
El Centro California
May 29, 2003

SCORING GUIDE

Student Self-Assessment	Teacher Assessment	
		ADVANCED (Expert)
✓		All items listed in proficient
✓		Plus: <u>diagrams of each water clock trial</u>
✓		Plus: diagrams and charts are <u>completely</u> labeled
✓		Plus: appropriate/advanced use of scientific language
		PROFICIENT
		4 of the following 5:
✓		Focus question relates to main idea of lesson
✓		A prediction that relates to the question
✓		A plan that relates to the question
✓		Data: Diagrams are clear and accurate
✓		Data: Diagrams of trials that worked/did not work
		All of the following –Claims and Evidence
✓		All claims are supported by evidence
✓		Descriptions/diagrams include correct labeling
✓		A chart with data from each trial
✓		What you learned
		PROGRESSING (Basic) 5-7 Proficient points
		DOES NOT MEET STANDARD (Far Below Basic) 4 or fewer Proficient Points

Assessing Student Progress

This assessment rubric provides the teacher with a means of examining a student science notebook entry for an individual lesson or for the entire unit of study. It is a means of identifying that the students have effectively used their science notebooks to form an understanding of the objective of the lesson or the big idea of the unit.

Another important principle that teachers need to remember is that metacognitive approaches to instruction can help students learn to define their own learning goals and monitor their own progress. It is equally important for teachers to keep in mind that metacognition is developmental and needs maturation, time, and practice. Teachers can best accomplish this by understanding what and how students are learning in science, a process of continuous assessment that must look at individual student growth as well as classroom trends that can be redirected through instruction as needed. Science instruction has the greatest impact on student learning when students can apply evidence from instructional experiences they have encountered to the knowledge they bring to the task and to the world surrounding them. When students have to explain their ideas about what they have learned and the way in which they are thinking about scientific processes, as is the case with science notebooks, they reinforce their learning experience. Students should understand the criteria for scoring, review their own work for completeness or revision, and comment on what they have learned. This is extremely important in an era of standards and accountability. Figure 14.2 (p. 101) is an example of a scoring rubric with a specific set of criteria.

This type of scoring rubric allows students to see the specific criteria or standard expected by the classroom teacher. This scoring rubric is distributed to the students prior to the lesson. In a class discussion, the teacher explains the criteria to the students. The expected target for all students should be at least "proficient." After students have completed the investigation, they are expected to use the scoring rubric to review their science notebook entries for completeness or revision. This type of rubric directly involves the students in the evaluation process through self-assessment.

These types of scoring rubrics involving students in self-assessment activities also can be summative in nature by offering a cumulative summary of achievement level for a series of lessons at the end of a unit or after a topic has been covered. These summative assessments of the student science notebook can serve several purposes: they help inform placement decisions and communicate a judgment about performance to parents and students. Many teachers are still required to assign a letter or number grade to their students, as opposed to determining their level of proficiency related to a set of standards. Figure 14.3 is an example of a scoring rubric developed by a fourth-grade teacher to assign point values to each of the components students were expected to record in their science notebooks. The students received a copy of the scoring rubric prior to the investigation, a classroom discussion took place whereby students were informed of the expectation for this lesson (criteria), and the

Figure 14.3

Grade 4 Scoring Rubric

Student Name: _____ Date: _____

Science Kit: Magnetism & Electricity   Lesson 5

Grade	Possible	Category Being Graded
	1	**Big Idea:**
	2	**Focus Question:** 🔥 One questions written clearly 🔥 Related to the scenario.
	5	**Prediction:** 🔥 One statement 🔥 Specifies the # of turns 🔥 Specifies where to put the wire 🔥 Specifies how to coil the wire 🔥 Uses "because"
	8	**Data:** 🔥 2 diagrams 🔥 Oersted's Observations 🔥 A chart for Oersted's Experiment 🔥 Complete and accurate 🔥 Labeled with titles 🔥 Washer experiment 🔥 A chart for washer experiment 🔥 Complete and accurate 🔥 Labeled with titles
	6	**Claims & Evidence:** 🔥 3 complete statements that answer guiding questions based on evidence
	2	**Conclusion:** 🔥 Accurately shows if prediction was supported or not and explains why
	1	**Reflection:** 🔥 Writes an investigable question using, "What would happen if . . ., and is related to the topic covered

_____ ÷ 25 = _____ Average Grade   Letter Grade Equivalent: _____

Teacher Comments: _____

_____

_____

_____

Assessing Student Progress

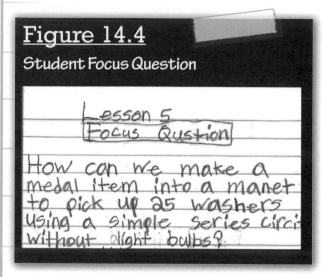

Figure 14.4

Student Focus Question

Lesson 5
Focus Qustion

How can we make a
medal item into a manet
to pick up 25 washers
using a simple series circi
without light bulbs?

students were asked to use the scoring rubric to examine their own science notebook entries before turning them in to the teacher.

The classroom teacher then used the scoring rubric to determine the degree to which the individual students met the criteria discussed prior to the lesson. Figure 14.4 is an example of a focus question from one student. The focus question was written clearly and related to the engaging scenario or problem (How can we make an electromagnet that will pick up 25 washers?) and was scored a "2" by the classroom teacher.

Figure 14.5 is another excerpt from the same student science notebook. As part of the conclusion, students were asked to return to their prediction to determine if it needed to be revised or affirmed. The student had predicted that if a current-carry-

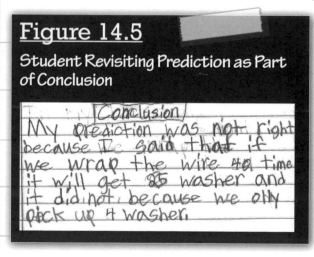

Figure 14.5

Student Revisiting Prediction as Part of Conclusion

Conclusion
My prediction was not right
because I said that if
we wrap the wire 40 time
it will get 25 washer and
it did not because we only
pick up 4 washer.

ing wire were wrapped around a rivet 40 times, it would pick up 25 washers. In this follow-up notebook entry the student indicated that it only picked up 4 washers. This met the criteria on the scoring rubric and was "scored" 2 points.

The teacher examined the entire class set of science notebooks looking for student understanding that the number of washers picked up was related to the number of winds of a current-carrying wire around an iron rivet. The teacher determined that the students had not clearly identified this relationship. In fact, the teacher noticed that the students were using a great number of winds of a current-carrying wire yet not picking up many washers. The teacher determined that the batteries that the students were using may have become very weak from frequent use in the unit and decided to have the students replicate their investigations using fresh batteries. After redoing the investigation, the teacher noted that fresh batteries made a great difference in the results and in developing correct student understanding. In this way the teacher used the science notebook as a formative assessment tool that informed her decision to have the students redo the investigation. Similar types of scoring rubrics may be created for all lessons in the unit, for essential lessons, or for embedded assessments.

Summative assessment only becomes formative in nature when either the teacher or the student uses the information to inform teaching or to influence learning. Then, data from summative assessments can be used in formative ways. In practice, if teachers frequently assess student notebooks, provide students with feedback that informs, and use class and individual progress to shape instruction, standards will be attained and students will develop a deep understanding of the science content.

Student science notebooks are the best record of what an individual student has actually learned during a lesson or an entire unit of study. As such, student science notebooks are effective formative and summative assessment tools. The range of understanding expected of students in the standards era is complex. Students must make connections among concepts just as scientists do, and then use that information in a specific context. This context involves problem-solving skills and procedural knowledge that requires students to work with data derived from an investigation. The focus on inquiry requires students to question, predict, plan, and conduct investigations, then analyze data and create evidence-based explanations and conclusions that may lead to new questions. In this context, the student science notebook is the most appropriate assessment tool for teachers to use in determining how successful students are at making meaning from their classroom science experience.

15 The Power of Feedback

As stated in Chapter 14, student science notebooks play an important role in the triad of what should be taught (standards), what is actually taught (classroom instruction), and what content students learn. The student science notebook is the best record of the depth of student content understanding and the quality of their communication of that understanding. When viewed as a formative assessment tool, the role of teacher feedback can play an important part in the development of student conceptual understanding and complex reasoning by students.

The Power of Feedback

One of the most important strategies a teacher can use is to provide students with feedback on their work. Teacher feedback is an important component in the process of using student notebooks in inquiry-based science instruction. Marzano et al. (2001) reported in a review of nine research studies that feedback that guides students rather than telling them what is right or wrong on an assessment can attain an effect size of .90 or higher. This translates into a shift forward of almost one standard deviation of change on a standardized test. In an era of high-stakes testing, this is important for teachers to consider when providing feedback. The most appropriate form of feedback for student science notebooks is asking guiding questions to the student or writing guiding questions in their science notebooks. The feedback can take the form of a personal written conversation between the teacher and the student in the student's science notebook. Teachers using student science notebooks as an assessment tool in their classrooms should stress this form of feedback with the understanding that the quality of the feedback is more important than the quantity of feedback. This form of feedback can best be summarized as "issues, evidence, and you." For example, the teacher may write:

What evidence do you have to support your claims?

What claims can you make from your evidence?

Is there another explanation for what happened?

The first guiding question of "What evidence do you have to support your claims?" is an important feedback point of reference. Many times students make claims that are not supported by the evidence collected in their investigation. Conversely the second reference point for feedback is found in the second guiding question, "What claims can you make from your evidence?" Many students use the evidence from their investigation to make claims that are based upon existing misconceptions and not on the data that was collected. Teachers may also consider assisting students in looking at other explanations for the observation or data that was collected. This assistance leads to the third guiding question, "Is there another explanation for what happened?"

The timing of feedback also appears to be critical to its effectiveness. Students generate many misconceptions regarding science concepts. In general, the more delay that occurs in giving feedback, the longer it takes students to clear misconceptions. Not only should feedback be timely, it should also reference a specific developmentally appropriate level of skill or knowledge expected of students. One way classroom teachers can assist students in moving their thinking toward "big ideas" in science is through the use of developmental "storylines." Developmental storylines serve as a graphic organizer that establishes a flowchart indicating the "big idea" or unifying concept of each unit of study (Amaral et al. 2002). These storylines then become the basis for the development of rubrics that can be used by teachers to provide appropriate written feedback to students in their science notebooks. Research on feedback also indicates that students can effectively monitor their own progress (Marzano et al. 2001). This is also an attribute of developing metacognitive thinking by students. A scoring rubric was introduced in Chapter 14 (Figure 14.2) that addresses this issue. This self-evaluating form of feedback is also important in the construction of meaning by the students.

Gaps between what was expected and what was accomplished are evidenced by comparing the guiding questions for the lesson to student entries in their notebooks. Gaps need to be communicated to the student with written corrective and content-based feedback. Equally important are written comments aimed at improving the quality of communication and level of conceptual understanding. Effective written feedback usually contains an action verb and serves to move students toward higher-level thinking skills. Student's whose science notebooks are not given written corrective feedback usually do not show quality of communication and conceptual understanding improvement over time and a significant number actually decline in quality of communication and understanding (Ruiz-Primo et al. 2002).

While most classroom teachers realize the significance of providing feedback to student work as an important aspect in the development of student quality of communication and conceptual understanding, many view the actual task of providing the feedback a daunting task. With large class sizes and other subjects to cover, many teachers find it difficult to provide feedback that is timely or even at all.

There are several strategies that classroom teachers can use to provide effective feedback, despite the constraints of time and magnitude. One strategy is for the teacher to use a pad of Post-Its as they circulate around the classroom during the science investigation. As classroom teachers circulate and observe student work, feedback notes can be written and stuck to the student science notebook. During class discussion, when students are sharing their framing questions, predictions, or plans, teachers can again write feedback comments on Post-It notes and then stick them in the student science notebooks. This strategy can also be used during class discussion when students are sharing claims linked to evidence and conclusions. Teachers can also divide the class into four groups and read the science notebooks from one group each week.

Teachers may also consider providing written feedback only for key or pivotal lessons. This will provide timely feedback to help dispel misconceptions and give immediate confirmation that the student is on target. Examples of pivotal lessons include lessons in magnetism and electricity where students are learning what is needed to make a simple circuit. Without this understanding, students will not be successful later in the unit learning about series and parallel circuits. Another example is in a unit on the properties of rocks and minerals. Without an

The Power of Feedback

understanding of the property of hardness, students will have great difficultly in the classification of minerals later in the unit.

Regardless of the method teachers use to provide feedback to students on the quality of communication and quality of conceptual understanding in their student science notebooks, written feedback must be given by teachers in order for students to deepen their understanding. The feedback must be descriptive and criterion-based and emphasize learning goals in order to lead to greater student understanding. Thus, the science notebook becomes a continuing record of student work and student progress. The written comments on student work that indicate a specific action to close the gap between the current student understanding and the desired outcome provide the student with information they can use to reach the desired outcome or accomplish a learning goal.

Teachers need to analyze and interpret student's responses to questions or their actions in problem-solving situations. Teachers then need to use the data from assessments in order to make inferences that form the basis for their feedback. The feedback conversation then is focused on the ways in which students can close the gap between their present understanding and the desired outcome held by the teacher.

Implications and Concluding Remarks

One of the teacher's primary roles in providing effective instruction in science is to have students communicate their thinking and development of ideas through the use of student science notebooks. The science notebook then becomes a written and visual representation of the communication of these ideas. Communication is vital to the developmental growth in learning for students. Student science notebooks can form the basis for an evolving student record of what they know. The student science notebook forms the basis for evidence-based classroom discussions where ideas are openly shared. It provides the basis for new investigations, invites the testing for new ideas, proposes possible explanations for current investigations and provides a pathway for new exploration for students.

Implications and Concluding Remarks

Student contributions to classroom discussion often are richer when drawn from the written record of the student science notebook. These contributions can also impact the thinking of other students within the class and solidify the thinking of the contributor and thus utilize higher-order thinking skills such as application, synthesis, and evaluation. Students can compare and contrast results with their peers.

Student science notebooks provide an evolving record of student thinking. They act as an extension of student thinking, a paper memory of personally derived information. They contain questions, drawings, cross-outs, and explanations, all of which become a part of the formative development of scientific reasoning on the part of the student. This is exactly how actual scientists use their own science notebooks, both as a tool to think and as a tool to communicate.

Teachers need to develop a relationship where students feel relaxed and confident with their work. Students need to be aware that they can communicate through their science notebook. Teachers can communicate with students through written feedback in the science notebook to provide encouragement or make suggestions on how students can clarify their thinking or organize their results. Student understanding can be increased through helpful teacher feedback. The earlier students start to use science notebooks, the better prepared they will be to make them an integral part of their science activities.

Often teachers become frustrated when students' written records in their science notebooks are incomplete or their drawing and illustrations are not as accurate as desired. How should the teacher react to this? Actually, the teacher should do nothing but provide feedback in the form of guiding questions, recognizing that communication is a developmental skill that requires practice. Feedback will guide the student to improve that practice.

Teachers must recognize that children need time to develop their skill in recording in their science notebooks in order to develop personal self-expression. Using the sentence starters and other strategies provided in this book should help guide students. With enough practice, student science notebooks will become useful instruments for students to record not only what they what they did in their investigations but most importantly what they learned. Science notebooks play a valuable role in science education for both the students and their teacher. They provide the best record of the students' ideas and interests and increase students' interest and ability in recording their work. They also provide the teacher with a means of assessing both student progress and the effectiveness of the instructional program. Science notebooks should have an integral role in science instruction, acting as a vital tool for both students and teachers in every step of an investigation, from beginning vocabulary discussions to the final assessment of what was learned.

r. References

Amaral, O., L. Garrison, and M. Duron-Flores. 2006. Taking inventory. *Science and Children* 43 (4): 30–33.

Amaral, O., L. Garrison, and M. Klentschy. 2002. Helping English learners increase achievement through inquiry-based science instruction. *Bilingual Research Journal* 26 (2): 213–239.

American Association for the Advancement of Science. 1993. *Benchmarks for science literacy*. New York, NY: Oxford University Press.

Aschbacher, P., and C. Baker. 2003. Incorporating literacy into hands-on science classes: Reflections in student work. Paper presented at the American Research Association Conference, Chicago, IL.

Black, P., and D. Wiliam. 1998. Inside the black box: Raising standards through classroom assessment. *Phi Delta Kappan* 80 (2): 139–148.

Campbell, B., and L. Fulton. 2003. *Science notebooks*. Portsmouth, NH: Heinemann.

Fellows, N. 1994. A window into thinking: Using student writing to understand conceptual change in science learning. *Journal of Research in Science Teaching* 31 (9): 985–1001.

Glynn, S., and D. Muth. 1994. Reading and writing to learn science: Achieving scientific literacy. *Journal of Research in Science Teaching* 31 (9): 1057–1073.

Hug, B., J. Krajcik, and R. Marx. 2005. Using innovative learning technologies to promote learning and engagement in urban science classrooms. *Urban Education* 40: 446–472.

Jorgenson, O., and R. Vanosdall. 2002. The death of science? What are we risking in our rush toward standardized testing and the three r's. *Phi Delta Kappan* 83 (8): 601–605.

Kleinsasser, A., E. Paradis, and R. Stewart. April, 1992. Perceptions of novices' conception of educational role models: An analysis of narrative writing. Paper presented at the Annual Meeting of the American Educational Research Association, San Francisco, CA.

Klentschy, M. 2005. Science notebook essentials. *Science and Children* 43 (3): 24–27.

References

Klentschy, M. 2006. Science education in a NCLB standards-based world. In *Linking science and literacy in the K–8 classroom*, eds. R. Douglas, M. Klentschy, and K. Worth, 373–390. Arlington, VA: NSTA Press.

Klentschy, M., and E. Molina-De La Torre. 2004. Students' science notebooks and the inquiry process. In *Crossing boarders in literacy and science instruction: Perspectives on theory and practice*, ed. W. Saul, 340–354. Newark, DE: International Reading Association.

Marzano, R., D. Pickering, and J. Pollock. 2001. *Classroom instruction that works: Research-based strategies for increasing student achievement*. Alexandria, VA: Association for Supervision and Curriculum Development.

Moline, S. 1995. *I see what you mean. Children at work with visual information*. Portland, ME: Stenhouse.

National Research Council (NRC). 1996. *National science education standards*. Washington, DC: National Academy Press.

National Research Council (NRC). 1999. *How people learn: Brain, mind, experience and school*. Washington, DC: National Academy Press.

National Research Council (NRC). 2000. *Inquiry and the national science education standards*. Washington, DC: National Academy Press.

National Research Council (NRC). 2001. *Classroom assessment and the national science education standards*. Washington, DC: National Academy Press.

National Research Council (NRC). 2005. *How students learn: History, mathematics and science in the classroom*. Washington, DC: National Academy Press.

Rivard, L. 1994. A review of writing to learn in science: implications for practice and research. *Journal of Research in Science Teaching* 31 (9): 969–983.

Rivard, L., and S. Straw. 2000. The effect of talk and writing on learning science: An exploratory study. *Science Education* 84 (5): 566–593.

Ruiz-Primo, A., M. Li, and R. Shavelson. 2002. Looking into student science notebooks: What do teachers do with them? CRESST Technical Report 562. Los Angeles, CA: CRESST.

Saul, W., J. Reardon, C. Pearce, D. Dieckman, and D. Neutze. 2002. *Science workshop: Reading, writing, and thinking like a scientist.* 2nd ed. Portsmouth, NH: Heinemann.

Scardamalia, M., and C. Bereiter. 1986. Research on written composition. In *Handbook on research on teaching* (3rd ed.), ed. Merlin C. Witrock, 778–803. New York: MacMillan.

Shepardson, D. 1997. Of butterflies and beetles: First graders' ways of seeing and talking about insect life cycles. *Journal of Research in Science Teaching* 34 (9): 873–889.

Shepardson, D., and S. Britsch. 2001. The role of children's journals in elementary school science activities. *Journal of Research in Science Teaching* 38 (1): 43–69.

Songer, N. 2003. Persistence of inquiry: Evidence of complex reasoning among inner-city middle school students. Paper presented at the Annual Meeting of the American Educational Research Association, San Diego, CA.

Songer, N., and P. Ho. 2005. Guiding the "explain": A modified learning cycle approach towards evidence on the development of scientific explanations. Paper presented at the Annual Meeting of the American Education Research Association, Montreal, Canada.

Vitale, M., N. Romance, and M. Klentschy. 2005. Enhancing the time allocated to elementary science by linking reading comprehension to science: Implications of a knowledge-based model. Paper presented at the Annual Meeting of the National Association of Research in Science Teaching, Dallas, TX.

Vygotsky, L. S. 1978. *Language and thought.* Cambridge: MIT Press.

White, B., and J. Fredrickson. 1998. Inquiry, modeling, and metacognition: Making science accessible to all students. *Cognition and Instruction* 16 (1): 42–56.

White, R., and R. Gundstone. 1992. *Constructing knowledge together: Classrooms as centers of inquiry and literacy.* Portsmouth, NH: Heinemann.

a. About the Author

Michael P. Klentschy is currently a faculty member in the College of Education at San Diego State University, Imperial Valley Campus. He served as superintendent of the El Centro School District in El Centro, California, for 14 years. He has also served in teaching and administrative positions in the Los Angeles Unified School District since the mid-1960s. Among his other honors is his naming by the National Science Education Leadership Association (NSELA) as 2005 Administrator of the Year.

i. Index

Index

Index

Index

Index

National Science Teachers Association

Index